OUR PROTESTANT HERITAGE

Our Protestant Heritage

A SERIES OF SERMONS

By
Harold John Ockenga
*Minister, Park Street Congregational Church,
Boston, Mass.*

WIPF & STOCK · Eugene, Oregon

Wipf and Stock Publishers
199 W 8th Ave, Suite 3
Eugene, OR 97401

Our Protestant Heritage
A Series of Sermons
By Ockenga, Harold John and Rosell, Garth M.
Copyright©1938 by Ockenga, Harold John
ISBN 13: 978-1-5326-1735-5
Publication date 1/25/2017
Previously published by Zondervan, 1938

TO MOTHER
WHO FIRST DEDICATED HER SON TO THE SERVICE
OF THE TRIUNE GOD AND THEN LED
HIM IN HIS PATHS

PREFACE

RECENTLY several critics scathed Protestantism in a very destructive manner. They planted seeds of doubt in the minds of those who are faithfully resisting the many disintegrating tendencies of modern life as they affect the Church. We consider this to be tragic, for they have substituted nothing constructive for the Church. They are destroying the foundations of the walls of Zion.

In reply to them we wish to reaffirm our great PROTESTANT HERITAGE. We submit that Protestantism is the fruit of a dialectic movement of over three hundred years, costing thousands of lives among those who believed. The fundamental conviction is ours that Protestantism is not "done" and that it is in no danger of complete disintegration, if the genius of Protestantism is understood.

A vigorous Protestantism emphasizing individualism, dissent, liberty, and tolerance is essential to combat the alien forces now operating in America. Protestantism is bound up with America's national heritage.

These modern church union movements are all wrong. They misunderstand the true nature of Protestantism. They are tending to create a second Roman church, perhaps not to compete with the first, but to bring about by uniformity the end of the dissenting mind. We have no quarrel with Romanism, but our mission is utterly different. Unity in Protestantism must not be organizational. Even denominations ob-

Preface

scure Protestantism's functioning. It is a time to reclaim the essential genius of Protestantism.

If Protestantism is dying, it is worthy to die. It has lost its cause for existence, its unique conceptions, its peculiar heritage. Our weakness has arisen from the act of stopping part way in a great dialectic movement of thought. In the proportion that Protestantism dies, the cardinal principles of American democracy die and we may expect the end of our present government, for America is the product of Protestantism.

Our purpose is to present this dialectic in the background of the ideology and biography of seven characters who were steps in this Protestant development. We make no claim to originality and have used available historical sources freely. If we speak derogatorily of any person or class of persons such as the Cavaliers or the Puritans, it is not from personal animosity, but because they were opponents of the dialectic movement.

The understanding of the genius of Protestantism will do more to awaken Protestants than anything else except a visitation of the Spirit of God, for which also we pray.

H. J. O.

Boston, Massachusetts.

CONTENTS

CHAPTER I
MARTIN LUTHER AND GERMANY 11
Reformation Truths

CHAPTER II
ULRICH ZWINGLI AND SWITZERLAND 27
Reformed Doctrine of the Communion

CHAPTER III
JOHN CALVIN AND GENEVA 51
The Truth of Predestination

CHAPTER IV
WILLIAM OF ORANGE AND THE NETHERLANDS 65
Christian Liberty

CHAPTER V
JOHN KNOX AND SCOTLAND 79
The Power of Conscience

CHAPTER VI
OLIVER CROMWELL AND ENGLAND 95
The Providence of God

CHAPTER VII
ROGER WILLIAMS AND AMERICA 111
The Genius of Protestantism

CHAPTER VIII
WHITHER PROTESTANTISM 127
Independency and Union

I
MARTIN LUTHER AND GERMANY
OR
REFORMATION TRUTHS

I

MARTIN LUTHER AND GERMANY
OR
REFORMATION TRUTHS

"That no man is justified by the law in the sight of God, it is evident: for, the just shall live by faith."

ONE decade of the sixteenth century set more forces in motion than any other in the last four hundred years. The dominating figure of those ten years was Martin Luther. The Reformation itself is closely connected with modern literature, education, prosperity, and political history, so that it has become the most important of modern historical changes. No one can claim to be well informed who is not acquainted with its leading issues and developments as it spread from Germany to Switzerland, France, the Netherlands, Sweden, England, and Scotland.

The Reformation time is most interesting. It dawned on Europe at the close of the Renaissance and was causally connected with it in no small degree. The Middle Ages, with their bondage of feudalism and their scholastic dialectic as an intellectual method, were breaking of their own weight. Controversies over names, the nature of angels, and little understood philosophical concepts had wearied the minds of men. Scholasticism insisted on authority; before a man was a recognized scholar he was compelled to be able to repeat the unending jargon of the schools. Then came the new birth of learning. In Italy there was a recrudescence of the intellectual spirit of ancient Greece and Rome, largely made possible through the contacts of the Crusades. A group of men interested in the humanities began the colossal task of collecting and editing ancient manuscripts and of placing the magnificent heritage of ancient culture at the disposal of modern life. Names such as Leonardo Bruni, Lorenzo Valla, Lorenzo the Magnificent, Giovanni Pico, Niccolo Machiavelli, and Cosimo de'Medici, were connected with that period. The fall of Constantinople drove numerous Greek scholars into Italy about 1453, and from them Greek humanism received a strong impetus. Inextricable from this intellectual movement was the transition from the Guild organization of commerce to the capitalistic system of modern times. A new society was created based upon the acquisition of wealth. Economic power passed to the hands of the individual, and the modern classes of bourgeoisie and proletariat were created. The year 1453 may be arbitrarily set as marking the beginning of the modern era.

It was some time later that the Renaissance learning spread to northern Europe, but when it did, names of scholars, such as Erasmus, Reuchlin, and Wolmar became prominent. These were the scholars who placed the instruments of learning in the hands of the Reformers, which made them able to reject the scholastic authority of Medievalism and return to the primitive sources of Christianity. Of no small import was the other factor developed and used in connection with the Renaissance and the Reformation—the printing press. It spread abroad these ideas into the cities and hamlets of Europe where they were avidly absorbed by intellectually hungry people.

The Renaissance blessings were not unmixed. Along with intellectual liberty came an intensification of moral depravity. Any historian candidly describes this. The sixteenth century was commenced under the control of the Roman Pontiff Alexander VI. Says Mosheim of him: "Alexander VI, whom humanity disowns and who is rather to be considered as a monster than as a man, whose deeds excite horror, and whose enormities place him on the level of the most execrable tyrants of modern times, stained the commencement of this century by the most atrocious crimes." He was followed by Julius II, who dishonored the pontificate with the most savage ferocity, the most audacious arrogance, the most despotic vehemence of temper, and the most extravagant passion for war and bloodshed. He kept Europe in a turmoil for ten years. Then came Leo X. He was remarkable for his prodigality, luxury, and cultural improvements, and has even been charged with impiety, if not atheism. Nevertheless, he was learned and patronized the arts, when he was not indulging in some immoral pleasure.

It was against such a church that Erasmus and others pointed the delicacy of their wit or leveled the fury of their indignation, and through writings, such as *The Praise of Folly*, undermined the superstitions of the times and the authority of Rome. The Emperor Maximilian I, with the help of some cardinals, attempted to reform the pontificate but failed. Maximilian was followed by Charles V, who was devoted to the church. The emperor held his crown at the will of the pontificate, and he required the support of the princes of the provinces and states to continue in power. One of these princes was Frederick, the Elector of Saxony, who later befriended Luther. In these domains of the empire the common people were groaning in their last struggle with feudalism. Their lot was deplorable, a literal slavery; the future held no hope for them; and when Luther's teaching concerning the value of the individual came to them, it fired an enthusiasm which seemed to promise deliverance. Some historians even to this day think that Luther should have gone farther and have emancipated the people from their material bondage.

Forerunners of the Reformation had not been lacking. Savonarola had boomed out in Florence against the iniquities of the Medicis and was a martyr to his cause. John Huss and the Bohemians had preached the doctrine of the authority of the Scriptures over against the pope and he had been burned at the stake. The Waldensians were true Protestants in all that that name later came to mean, but were so worked upon by the Inquisition and the sword that they were all but blotted out. The Beghards were entirely suppressed. Fire, sword, and Inquisition rendered the remnants of these Protestant movements so feeble that they were scorned rather than persecuted. Yet widely disseminated was the princely and common opposition to the tyranny of the papacy. Said one historian: "Ministers who would have taken it into their heads to inculcate the doctrines and precepts of the gospel, to exhibit the example of its divine Author, and the efficacy of its mediation, as the most powerful motives to righteousness and virtue, and to represent the love of God and mankind as the great duties of the Christian life, would have been very unprofitable servants to the church and to the papacy, however they might have promoted the cause of virtue and the salvation of souls. . . . Proportionate to the greatness of this corruption of the church was the impatient ardor with which all who were endowed with any tolerable portion of solid learning, genuine piety, or even good sense, desired to see the church reformed and purged from these shocking abuses." Then occurred the incident that kindled the flames of the Reformation.

I. THE REFORMATION LEADER

Early in 1517 a Dominican monk named John Tetzel came to Saxony. He was the representative of Leo X, who was in great need of money. Leo was a connoisseur of pictures and statues and he wanted to complete St. Peter's Church, which was a crowning glory of papal magnificence. He also squandered vast revenues in pleasures and pomps. Kings and bishops were getting tired of the everlasting drain of money to Rome. So Leo revived an old custom. He would sell indulgences for sin and send agents to peddle them in every country. Tetzel was the agent in the country of Luther. He had been chosen because of his uncommon impudence to preach and proclaim in Germany the indulgence which administered the remission of all sins, past, present, and to come, however enormous their nature, to those who were rich enough to purchase them. Tetzel was inordinately affronting and not only was guilty of matchless insolence, but went so far as to derogate the all-sufficient power and merits of Christ. That Tetzel acted on the authority of the church is proved by a later command of Cardinal Cajetan to Luther to believe on the dictates of the church that "one drop of Christ's blood being sufficient to redeem the whole race, the remaining quantity, which was shed in the garden and on the cross, was left as a legacy to the church, to be a treasure whence indulgences were to be drawn and administered by the Roman pontiff."

With just indignation Luther raised his voice of warning and preached against Tetzel and the abominable traffic of indulgences. Only God can forgive sins. These indulgences made a mockery of virtue. It was necessary to assail the principles upon which they were based. Everybody had believed that penance would insure salvation, and these were a form of penance. Penance consisted in a temporal penalty inflicted on the sinner after a confession to the priest as a condition of his receiving an authoritative pardon of his sin. The indulgence was an official remission of this penalty gained by offerings of money made to the church for official uses. To attack these and to instruct his students and people Martin Luther drew up his celebrated ninety-five theses. Thus was struck the first blow of the Reformation.

Who was this Luther? His origin was extremely humble, being born of poor peasants and reared in penury. He was even an obscure and inconsiderable person when he came into public view in the indulgence controversy. His education took place in the common schools in Mansfield and Magdeburg and Eisenach, and later in the University of Erfurt, where he distinguished himself. He sang his way through, and soon entered an Augustinian monastery, there pursuing his studies. He earned several advanced degrees and was appointed professor of divinity in the University of Wittenberg, then recently erected by Elector Frederick. We shall say something of Luther's spiritual struggles later, but personally he was just the man for the work of the Reformation. He was "sprung from the people, poor, popular, fervent; educated amid privations, religious by nature, yet with exuberant animal spirits, dogmatic, boisterous, intrepid, with a great insight into realities; practical, untiring, learned, generally cheerful and hopeful, emancipated from the terrors of the Middle Ages; progressive in his spirit, lofty in his character, earnest in his piety, believing in the future and in God." None of the pictures or statues so common in Germany represent Luther as a refined looking man, but rather as coarse and sensual. But he possessed a bold fortitude with deep convictions and rapid intellectual processes. He was kind-hearted, generous, and brave. He was a man of the people and had he been more polished, fastidious, and modest, he could never have faced the demands of his herculean undertaking. Mosheim describes him: "His genius was truly great and unparalleled, his memory vast and tenacious; his patience in supporting trials, difficulties, and labor, incredible; his magnanimity invincible, and unshaken by the vicissitudes of human affairs; and his learning most extensive, considering the age in which he lived." The people loved Luther for his broad humanity. They never loved the monks. They feared them. But Luther was human; the people felt that he was one of them.

When Luther had thoroughly worsted Tetzel in the controversy and had stirred Germany with his theses, the schools took up the controversy. The pope took knowledge of it and sent one of the most learned men to debate with and silence this German monk. They met in the great hall in a palace at Leipsic. Doctors of theology, church dignitaries, statesmen, and electors gathered to hear the debate. Dr. Eck was superior in dialectical skill and scholastical learning and he overwhelmed Luther with his quotations from Catholic writers, literature of the church, and decrees of councils.

When he thought he had vanquished Luther, the debate took a different turn, for the German monk brushed aside all secondary authority and appealed directly to the Scriptures as the final authority. These he knew as few others of his day. The result of the debate was that Luther won the support of the Elector Frederick and of the common people, which was an essential factor in his success. Moreover, Luther was forced in his own thinking to realize that the church was thoroughly wrong in its emphasis on the authority of tradition, and that many of its teachings were contrary to the Bible. Dr. Eck appealed to the pope, and Leo took a direct hand in the proceedings.

The first notice that the pope took of Luther was at the time he nailed his theses to the door of the church in Wittenberg. Leo was struck with their power. Said he, "This Dr. Luther is a man of fine genius." Later when Luther's living words had stirred students and people as by Pentecostal fires, the pope took a different interest. He dispatched Eck to refute him, and when this failed, he commanded Cardinal Cajetan to silence him; but this was a mistake for the cardinal was an arrogant, egotistic, prejudiced Dominican, to whom Luther would never submit. Cajetan insisted that Luther renounce his opinions without trying to refute him. When this failed, Charles Miltitz, a Saxon knight, was dispatched to suavely influence Luther by an offer of a cardinal's cap and great honor. The results of the efforts by diplomatic Miltitz consisted in Luther's agreement to be silent as long as his enemies were. But when they openly attacked him the controversy broke out afresh, and the papal excommunication of the German monk soon followed.

II. THE REFORMATION TRUTHS

Governing ideas are few. Their discovery usually results in the birth of a dynamic movement. Three governing ideas moved the Reformation. First, there was justification by faith. John Lord, the historian, said, "I wish to show what is historically true and clear; and I defy all the scholars and critics of the world to prove that this doctrine is not the basal pillar of the reformation of Luther. I wish to make emphatic the statement that justification by faith was, as an historical fact, the great primal idea of Luther; not new, but new to him and his age." In the discovery of this truth Luther went back to the teaching of the Bible.

I have followed in personal journeys the entire career of Luther, from his birthplace at Eisleben, through Eisenach, where he stayed in the home of Frau Cotta while he attended the local school; to the University of Erfurt and the Black Cloister of the Augustinian monastery where he flagellated himself, did penance, fasted, prayed, and studied his Bible; on his pilgrimage to the south; in the university halls, where he lived and taught in Wittenberg; along his trip to Worms, where he was tried before the Diet; back to Wartburg Castle in the forest of Thuringen, where he was held captive for a year; at Augsburg, where the great Lutheran confession was written; back to Wittenberg, where he taught and conducted the Lutheran movement; and finally to the little village of Eisleben, where he triumphantly passed into the world beyond and where he had been born. But to me the most sacred of all places and that most meaningful to modern Christianity is the Black Cloister at Erfurt, where after years of struggle and search for peace Luther, through the study of the Books of Romans and Galatians, apprehended the truth of justification by faith. Once he understood and experienced this truth, based upon the grace of a sovereign God, he discovered that it was the foundation of the apostolic fathers' and the Augustinian theology. Taking his stand upon it, he found that he could challenge with impunity the most able opponents of his position.

Men deny that truth was the basis for the Reformation and sneeringly say that it came from Luther's desire to marry Catherine von Bora. But the genius of the Reformation was religious, and its strength rested in this new and yet old idea of salvation, the idea of Paul, of Augustine, of Huss, of Wycliffe; it consisted in the declaration of salvation by a belief in the incarnate Son of God shedding His blood for the sins of the world. Herein was manifested the love of God. The idea was sufficient to sweep through Europe, to wipe away the practice of penance, to convince the people that they had been pagan, and to lead them to search the Bible and become vocal in their praises of Christ as their deliverer, King, and Lord. Not only Germany, but Switzerland, France, England, and Scotland seized upon the idea and let it become the source of distinctive ruggedness of character.

The second idea stated by Luther, but taught in the Bible, is the supreme authority of the Scriptures. Luther did not deny other authorities, but he claimed that authority in its highest form as the last court of appeal rests in the Holy Scriptures, in the writings of Peter and Paul, in the teachings of Jesus, in the whole Bible. This laid the cornerstone of Protestantism. It is true that Protestants differ as to the meaning of certain texts and thereby denominational divisions have arisen, but the Bible has always been the authority of

Protestantism. And it is to be interpreted by learning and reason. The two great attacks upon this Protestant doctrine have been from the Roman Catholics and rationalists. The Catholics undermine the teaching of the Bible by invalidating it through tradition and unscriptural practices. Catholicism says, "We accept the Bible, but we do not believe the common people are able to interpret it. It is a sealed book except to the learned and therefore must be kept only in the hands of the clergy. If the common people have the Bible they will become fanatics and will get notions fatal to the authority of the church." Rationalism, which has become prominent in the last century, rejects the plain and obvious teachings of the Scripture as inconsistent with reason and as uninspired. Man's reason must be supreme. This has done more harm than the Romanist theory. The Scriptures are the treasury of the divine truth for humanity, and they were recovered for the common man through the Reformation.

The third idea of Luther arose out of the teaching of the church that the Bible must not be entrusted to the private man. Luther insisted on the right of private judgment concerning the Bible. He believed that the Scriptures could be understood by the average man, that they were the light of life and the guide to heaven. He claimed that they were the only effective protection against superstition, and he preached the duty of spreading them so that every man may interpret them for himself according to the light that he has. He proclaimed spiritual liberty and obedience to the voice of individual conscience. He not only preached this but he translated the Bible into the German and gave it to the people for the first time in German history, thereby incidentally creating the German tongue. This point is the vital difference between Roman Catholicism and Protestantism. Many Romans accept the Augustinian ideas of grace and the supreme authority of the Scriptures, but rarely does a Roman tolerate religious liberty. Such would be a vital blow to the supremacy of their hierarchy. This individual liberty was the spiritual idea which actuated William of Orange in his contest against the murderous Duke of Alva, who by the execution of thousands of Netherlanders attempted to crush the Reformation. It actuated the Huguenots of France against Charles IX, the Separatists of England, the Scottish heroes following Knox, and it was the motivating power of American Protestantism. On its broad platform, which was the Bible itself, greatly contrasted characters could stand together.

III. THE REFORMATION DRAMA

Climatic in the drama of the decade beginning 1517 were several events. First was the day the lone, obscure monk and professor walked out of his study, down the main thoroughfare of Wittenberg to the castle church where with bold strokes he nailed his scroll of ninety-five theses challenging all comers to debate. It was truth and conviction of that truth shaking the world. A lone monk challenging the supreme power of the nations. Henry IV, emperor of Germany, had once been compelled to stand for three days in the snow before being admitted to the pope's presence to make repentance. But this German professor challenged the pope's power. Those theses attacked the visible head of the church to whom common belief ascribed the power of the spirit and of the sword.

The next incident in that powerful drama was the burning of the papal bull of excommunication. When

Luther was commanded to recant within sixty days or be apprehended by state authorities, which meant death, and the papal bull bringing the announcement to him was delivered, he convoked an assembly of students and townspeople outside the limits of Wittenberg, had an enormous pile of logs assembled, and there in a dramatic moment amid the cheers of the people consigned the document to the flames. By his action he renounced the authority of the church and broke with the church, although he did not withdraw from the greater Church, claiming rather that he was a member of it. This was the beginning of Protestantism.

Next came the Diet in the city of Worms. There gathered the emperor Charles V, the cardinals representing the pope, the archbishops and bishops, the electors and princes, and the doctors of the law. Luther was guaranteed safe conduct and was under the protection of his friend, Elector Frederick. He was asked to recant his writings, and a long speech was made against him. After twenty-four hours of interim, during which he was given time to think it over, the assembly reconvened and in a dramatic moment of great intensity, Luther was commanded to recant. He answered, "Unless you refute me by arguments drawn from the Scriptures, I cannot and will not recant anything . . . here I stand; I cannot otherwise: God help me! Amen." Without fear Luther had faced the supreme authority of those who had power to kill the body but had no power over the soul.

The next day friends accompanied Luther out of the city and started him secretly on his journey to Wittenberg. Suddenly in the Thuringen Forest four knights set upon him and kidnapped him. Friends thought that he had been killed. Foes knew not what had happened to him. His friend Frederick had dispatched these knights to hide him in the Wartburg castle for protection against papal emissaries. There he stayed for eleven months, translating the Bible, until he could hold himself no longer, and suddenly returned to Wittenberg to assume the leadership of the Protestant movement.

We are not particularly interested in nor can we say much about his marriage to Catherine von Bora or his subsequent life. It was filled with joys, dangers, temptations, and labors until he passed triumphantly through the gates of death in that upper room in Eisleben. Martin Luther was one of the great lights of history. He was a man who touched the rock of reality in spiritual things, and we believe those principles are true.

Like a mighty conflagration these truths were kindled in the minds of men in other countries in the following decades. We shall speak of them by and by. They become the broad basis of Protestant development and the underlying principles of a new era in Christian history. How strange it is that these are the truths being repudiated in the Protestant church today! Justification by faith is being superseded by a religion of ethics or of works. The authority of the Scriptures is being supplanted by the counsels of men; and the individual liberty, or the right of private judgment, is even being denied in the great Protestant succession. Nevertheless, we believe that the Reformation was right and on those principles and those governing ideas drawn directly from the Scriptures we shall take our stand in the face of all opposition and tendencies today.

ULRICH ZWINGLI AND
SWITZERLAND
OR THE
REFORMED DOCTRINE OF
THE COMMUNION

II

ULRICH ZWINGLI AND SWITZERLAND
OR THE
REFORMED DOCTRINE OF THE COMMUNION

"It is the Spirit that quickeneth; the flesh profiteth nothing: the words that I speak unto you, they are spirit, and they are life."

ULRICH ZWINGLI is second only to Martin Luther in the list of reformers. Luther may have had more drama connected with his Reformation, which is able to thrill men, but it is the quiet, reasoned progression of Zwingli's mind and logic that kindles the flame in my soul. The sweet pervasiveness of Zwingli's intellectual processes, devoted unreservedly to the cause of Christ, are to some of us more winning than the thundering denunciations of the German Reformation. Granting Zwingli's weaknesses, which we shall not pass over, we personally feel more in common with this truly great man and preacher than with any other of the Reformation leaders. We can follow him almost completely. God has His times and His seasons and He prepares His men for them. Just as God had chosen the new University of Wittenberg in Germany to be the heart of the Reformation activity under Luther's teaching, so He prepared under the best of teachers in several places and in different pastorates the Swiss preacher, Zwingli, that he might be ready for the hour of reform in his country. The times made the men, and they produced simultaneously Luther and Zwingli.

There are three phases to the Swiss Reformation. The first was 1519-1526, during which Zurich was the center and Zwingli the leader. The second was 1526-1532, with the center at Berne under the leadership of William Farel. In 1532, Geneva became the focus of the light of the Reformation, and John Calvin was the moving spirit. We shall speak of Calvin later. Farel's work we shall omit, but we should also recognize that there were many other contemporary reformers in Switzerland, such as Oswald Myconius, John Hausshein, known as Oecolampadius, or "the light of the house," Berthold Haller, Leo Juda, Henry Bullenger, and others. These were all outstanding men; but towering above them as an high peak of the Alps was Ulrich Zwingli.

Zwingli was a handsome man, of graceful manners, of pleasing conversation, of celebrated eloquence, and of rich genius. He loved music and was a master of several instruments. He was enthusiastic over art and increased the taste for it wherever he was. He had a lively disposition, and amiable character, and attractive conversational powers. He was kind, self-sacrificial, and devoted to charity. His person and manner often won over adversaries to his cause by means of moderation when his arguments failed.

Zwingli was born high up in the mountains of Switzerland. In the center of this beautiful land lies the Tockingberg Valley. On the north are the lofty mountains of the Sentis, which separate the valley from the canton Appenzel. On the south are the Kuhfirsten, with seven peaks rising between the Tockingberg Valley and the Wallen See. On the east the valley slopes away to the rising sun and displays the magnificent prospect of the Tyrolese Alps. On the highest portion

Ulrich Zwingli and Switzerland

of this elevated valley, two thousand feet above the level of Lake Zurich, lay a village named Wildhaus. On the outskirts was a peasant's cottage with thin walls, small windows enclosed with round panes of glass, shingled roof loaded with stone to prevent its being carried away by the wind, and other indications of antiquity. Here on New Year's Day, 1484, seven weeks before the birth of Martin Luther in Germany, a third son was born to the Amman of Wildhaus, by name Zwingli. The child was christened Ulrich.

Switzerland was then divided into cantons, or districts, each of which had a prominent city that dominated the district. The government was democratic. The cantons were bound together into a federation and the people were famed for their ability in war because of bravery. Often they hired themselves out as mercenaries to the monarchs of Europe. War became the profession of these Helvetic men, but from the wars in France and Italy they brought back many vices. Naturally they were honest, faithful, true, and capable of wonderful friendship, but these expeditions in foreign armies infused a reckless spirit into the people and a weakness toward immorality. An illustration of their licentiousness may be found in an incident in the life of one of the humble and quiet gentlemen of the reformers. He was a schoolmaster and though possessed of a scanty income had married a young woman whose purity of mind won the admiration of all. One day in winter during Oswald's absence a band of returned ruffians attacked his quiet dwelling. They smashed the windows, commanded his wife in indecent language, broke everything they could find, and then retired. When Oswald returned his son Felix ran to meet him with loud cries and his wife, unable to speak, made signs of her condition. The schoolmaster saw the rioters, seized a weapon, and pursued them into the cemetery. There three of them fell upon him and wounded him and then once again broke into his house with furious cries. This situation was to affect the life of Ulrich Zwingli as powerfully as the solitary mountains which watched over his home like silent sentinels.

The early youth of Ulrich was spent in joyous play in the presence of huge masses of rock. One of his friends later said, "I have often thought that being brought near to heaven on those sublime heights he there contracted something heavenly and divine." Zwingli's brothers were shepherds, and he was at first marked for the same life, but his father noticed that he was a promising lad intellectually and thus took him to visit an uncle who was dean at Wessen. At ten years of age, he showed such superior intellectual grasp that his uncle sent him to St. Theodore's school at Basel. This school he soon outgrew, and he went to the University of Berne. He became versed in classical learning of his day and then studied for a season in Vienna. Here he was educated in letters. Shortly afterward he took the degree of Master of Arts and returned to Berne to take up divinity. Even here his education did not cease, however, for he determined to learn Greek. He felt that divinity was largely a waste of time because of the scholastic controversies of his day; so he visited Erasmus and received great inspiration to pursue the classics.

At the age of twenty-two Zwingli was appointed to the large parish of Glaris, which was not far from his native home. He had already attracted the attention of the church by his learning and he received a pension

Ulrich Zwingli and Switzerland

which he turned to further studies. He immediately began to preach. Zwingli's ministry took place in three locations—Glaris, Einsiedeln, and Zurich. In Glaris he distinguished himself by his attack on the practice of sending mercenaries to fight the battles of other countries. He even went with two groups of these mercenaries as chaplain and beheld both their slaughter and the effect of Italy's contaminating morals. At Glaris he began to grasp some of the great truths of the Bible. As soon as he read the New Testament in Greek he was convinced of the grand principle of evangelical Christianity, namely, the infallible authority of the Holy Scriptures. This was one of the most fruitful periods of Zwingli's thinking, for he received time to acquaint himself with the Scriptures. After six years he was offered the position of priest and preacher at the famous shrine of Our Lady of Einsiedeln. To this shrine, which was supposed to have particular virtue in the remission of sins for those who made pilgrimages to it, came unnumbered pilgrims, who listened to the preacher, presented their offerings, made their petitions, and returned to their homes. Zwingli saw the great possibility of preaching to this multitude, representative of all Switzerland, and at the same time of devoting himself to study and meditation. Here he remained for three years, during which he openly criticized the background of Roman thinking and practice and was thoroughly prepared for his great and important work in Zurich, to which he was called when thirty-five years of age. He preached his first sermon in the cathedral on his thirty-fifth birthday. He remained as pastor of the Zurich church for the rest of his life, dying at the age of forty-eight. Had it not been for the years in the Hermit's Retreat in Einsiedeln, high in the Alps, Zwingli would not have been prepared for the responsibility of the Swiss reformation.

The religious convictions of Zwingli developed gradually. He did not arrive at the truth like Luther, by those storms which impel the soul to run hastily to its harbor of refuge. Zwingli reached the knowledge of the truth through the peaceful influence of the Scriptures, whose power gradually expands the heart. D'Aubigne says that Luther obtained the wished for shore through the storms of the wide ocean, but Zwingli by gliding softly down the stream. These are the two principal ways in which the Almighty leads men. It was only gradually that the glimmering rays of light simmered through the error of Zwingli's day and later cast the full light of the sun of truth upon him. As early as 1514 Zwingli prayed to God for an understanding of His Word, but it was not until 1522 that he was fully converted to God and the Bible.

Zwingli had never received from Rome the kind of treatment which had been administered to Luther. Rome had tried to frighten Luther by her doctors of the law, her councils, bishops, papal bulls, and excommunications. Rome offered to Zwingli her gold and her splendor. She bestowed upon him benefices, pensions, and honor. She gave him free communication with bishops and cardinals. Her dignitaries even came to confer with him while at Einsiedeln and promised reformation in the church. It was Rome's desire to hold Zwingli and the powerful Swiss cantons on her side because of the endless wars in which she was involved. This policy was far more skillful than that adapted to Luther but it was no more successful in silencing the tongue of Zwingli than had been that applied to Luther. Zwingli did not attack the church openly until he was

Ulrich Zwingli and Switzerland

forced to do so when the bishop turned against him because of his preaching against the indulgences proclaimed in Switzerland by Samson as they were by Tetzel in Germany. After this break Zwingli and the church separated.

A unique factor in Zwingli's career was his belief that he had a perfect right to rule in the state as well as in the church. He forgot the Scriptural text, "They who take the sword shall perish by the sword," and Jesus' words, "My kingdom is not of this world." Zwingli wielded the sword. He fought when he was a chaplain with the confederate mercenaries and he carried the sword in the disastrous battle of Cappel in which he was killed. Zwingli as a minister and preacher was heard with respect and obedience by most, but as a political leader and head of the army he wrought confusion among the Reformation forces in Switzerland. There is much to be said in support of Zwingli's action, for he was not as yet emancipated from the Roman idea that the church should wield the physical as well as the spiritual sword. Moreover, Rome was killing the evangelical priests and he believed that it was necessary to force the Catholic cantons to permit liberty for evangelicals. But as we see Zwingli lying beheaded on the fields of Cappel, only to be quartered and burned by his enemies, we realize afresh that the church has its place in spiritual matters only.

I. The Swiss Reformation

The Reformation in Switzerland was totally independent from the Lutheran movement in Germany. One historian says that the only connecting link between Luther and Zwingli must be looked for in heaven. He who gave the truth to Luther gave it to Zwingli also. Zwingli began to preach the gospel in 1516, before Luther was ever heard of in Switzerland. He had learned the doctrine of the gospel from the Word of God, which he had studied diligently in the original languages. Later when asked about Luther, Zwingli said, "If Luther preaches Christ, he does what I am doing... I will bear no other name than that of Christ, whose soldier I am, and who alone is my chief. Never has one single word been written by me to Luther nor by Luther to me." These two movements were to have influence upon each other, but they were utterly independent in their origin. In fact, Germany did not communicate the light of the truth to Switzerland or to France or to England. All these countries received it from God. One part of the world does not communicate the light of day to another. It is the same brilliant orb which imparts it to all the earth. Thus it was that Christ, the "dayspring from on high," at the era of the Reformation became the divine fire from which emanated the light of the world. The Reformation in these countries was a bursting forth of primitive Christianity in its full strength after having been obscured by paganism in the church for nearly twelve centuries.

We might contrast Zwingli and Luther. Zwingli was not interested in exposing the sores of the church. He simply was manifesting the lessons of the Bible to his flock as he understood them. He believed that if the people understand what is true they will soon discern what is false. Concerning the abuses of the day Luther had been enlightened by his pilgrimage to Rome, but Zwingli saw these at work in his own church at the shrine of Our Lady in Einsiedeln. Finally even

Ulrich Zwingli and Switzerland

Zwingli resolved to attack the evils of the church openly. Zwingli and Luther were different in their reasoning processes. They held the same faith but depended upon different reasoning. Luther acted on impulse, whereas Zwingli followed the clearness of argument. The entire Lutheran reformation came out of Luther's private convictions of the value of the Cross, whereas Zwingli was attracted by the harmony of Christian doctrine, by its exquisite beauty, and by the everlasting light which it brings into the world. Luther was governed somewhat by German mysticism, whereas Zwingli followed dialectic. Their attitudes concerning the church and the state differed, as we shall have reason to comment on later, as did also their soul struggles toward the truth.

This independence reflects the differences in the nations. One was monarchic and the other democratic. Hence in Germany there was one great reformer. In Switzerland there was a confederacy of reformers. In Germany, men were shocked into thinking by Luther's exposure of abuses. In Switzerland, they were led with moderation to an understanding of what is right. Both movements arose from a dire need of the reform of Romanism, the evils of which had reached the state which men could no longer endure.

Switzerland, by its democratic government, gave place to public debate and disputation. Consequently there really existed a freedom of speech and a willingness to hear who was right and could prove his position on the basis of reason and of the Scripture. When Zwingli was called to Zurich he began to preach all the great truths of Protestantism, but he was still within the church. He was a Roman priest, honored for his intellectual acumen and his influence among the people.

On the basis of his study of the Bible he repudiated many of the practices of the church. When Zwingli heard of the Lutheran controversy he placed the weight of his personal influence to lessen papal persecution of Luther. Zwingli's preaching brought results from the people. They embraced the truth and they renounced the Roman practices in great numbers. Opposition, however, was not lacking. Zwingli and a group of his colaborers in the ministry drew up sixty-seven theses and challenged any and all comers to refute them. A series of public discussions and debates took place, first at Zurich, then at Berne, then at Baden, and again at Zurich. The Roman defenders, for the most part, absented themselves from these discussions. When they did present themselves Zwingli, Haller, Oecolampadius, and others completely overcame them with arguments from the Scriptures. Finally, the Romanists refused even to come to the debates. There was a remarkable disposition in these debates for men, once they had been convinced of the truth, to embrace it. Such was Francis Lambert, who came to Zurich. He was preaching in the cathedral when suddenly a voice was heard saying, "Brother, you are mistaken." It was Zwingli. A day was set to debate the question. After both had presented their arguments Lambert suddenly stated that he was convinced of the truth as presented by Zwingli and he abandoned his former position and embraced the truth. Similarly, the councils who dominated the city government listened to the arguments of the pastors and then for the most part obeyed the Scriptural teaching.

What a preacher Zwingli was! Eloquently and convincingly he presented the truth so that hundreds of the clergy and multitudes of the people were converted.

Ulrich Zwingli and Switzerland

City after city declared for the Reformation as a result of these debates. The supreme truth that he presented, namely, that God alone is the source of salvation and He is everywhere, was sufficient to destroy many of the Romanist doctrines. No bolder action can be imagined than that of this preacher when he was a priest at the shrine of Our Lady in Einsiedeln. He addressed the multitude that came with these words, "Do not imagine that God is in this temple more than in any other part of the creation. Whatever be the country in which you dwell, God is around you and hears you as well as at Our Lady's at Einsiedeln. . . . Christ, who was once offered on the cross, is the sacrifice that has made satisfaction for the sins of the believer to all eternity." The multitudes hearing this turned back and those who met them did not even take the trouble to climb the mountain to the shrine. Zwingli's conviction shook the nations. At Zurich he did the unheard of thing of first making an explanation from his pulpit, verse by verse, of the books of the Bible, such as Matthew, Acts, and Hebrews. He was supported by the teacher Myconius and by his fellow-preachers.

II. THE DOCTRINE OF THE SWISS REFORM

The teachings of the Swiss Reformation were largely the same as the Lutheran. The first emphasis in thought was upon the Scriptures as the living testimony of truth in the heart. Thus the Bible became the source of the Swiss Reformation. This was the formal cause of the Reformation in every country. From the Scripture other truths were derived. Zwingli studied the celebrated doctors, such as Origen, Ambrose, Jerome, Augustine, and Chrysostom, but he did not study them as authorities. He simply sought their advice on certain passages of the Scripture. There were two dictums which routed the papists in all discussions. The first was that the Scripture was the ultimate authority. The second was that Scripture must be interpreted by Scripture, obscure pages by those that are clear. The Roman system could never be justified from the Bible. Zwingli even went farther than this. He believed that the individual must have the Holy Ghost as the interpreter of the Word. He found that his classical knowledge of philosophy and divinity were always raising objections to the teaching of the Word so that he determined to neglect those matters and look for God's will in His Word alone. He then determined to bring his life entirely into subjection to the will of God by obedience. He even committed to memory the epistles of St. Paul and many other portions of both the New Testament and the Old.

In singling out the truths of the Swiss Reformation we shall mention three as the source of other truths. Zwingli preached the sovereignty of God, the Saviorhood of Christ, and the spiritual nature of the church. Thinking of the sovereignty of God, Zwingli concluded that God is universally present, all powerful, the exclusive Creator, and the Lord of all. Roman Catholicism had permitted the doctrine of God to degenerate; and Zwingli called men back to this fundamental truth. From this he derived the truth of predestination. Often he called to the people who were irresolute and timid in loud accents of invitation, saying, "Are you afraid to approach this tender Father who has elected you? Why has He chosen us for His grace? Why has He called us? Why has He drawn us to Him? Is it that we should fear to approach Him?" Moreover, Zwingli

Ulrich Zwingli and Switzerland

believed because of predestination that such men of heathen times as Pindar, Plato, and the two Catos were saved because they were so high-minded and so earnestly desirous of knowing the truth. Because of election he was convinced that children born of believing parents are children of God and should be baptized as their parents and then trained in the Christian faith. From the doctrine of predestination he also received the doctrine of the fall. In this he had the key to the history of the human race. He realized that before the fall man had been created with a free will so that had he been willing he might have kept the law, but since he desired to be as God, he died, and not he alone, but all his posterity. All men in Adam are now dead and no man can recall them to life until the Spirit, who is God Himself, raises them from the dead. It was because Zwingli had a true knowledge of God that he understood the nature of man.

Central in all of Zwingli's preaching was the person of Christ. He believed that the life of Christ had been too long hidden from the people; hence he began his ministry in the cathedral with an exposition of the life of Jesus directly from the Scriptures. He consecrated his ministry to the praise of the only Son of God, who was able to save men's souls. Said he, to his crowded cathedral audience, "It is to Christ that I desire to lead you; to Christ the true source of salvation; His divine Word is the only food that I wish to set before your hearts and souls." Often Zwingli trembled because of his sinfulness, but he found in Christ a deliverance from every fear. Said he, "When Satan frightens me by crying out, 'You have not done this or that which God commands,' forthwith the gentle voice of the Gospel consoles me by saying, 'What thou canst not do Christ has done and perfected . . . Christ is thy innocence. Christ is thy righteousness. Christ is thy salvation. Thou art nothing. Thou canst do nothing. Christ is all things. He can do all things.'" He preached that Christ, who was once offered upon the cross, had made satisfaction for the sins of believers to all eternity. Somehow, however, when Zwingli was visited by the plague through ministering to his suffering people, Christ became even more to him. He became life itself—the sustaining and quickening power of his very existence. This is the same gospel which we preach, and like Zwingli, we believe it is independent of the church organization.

Zwingli had a doctrine of the church which was not that of a material organization. In the midst of his preaching he suddenly broke off and pointed to two humble Swiss sitting near him and said, "These are the church. Wherever two or three are met together in His name there the church is." The church for Zwingli was not a succession of popes, cardinals, and priests with an idolatrous mass, but the body of Christ. He proclaimed that the church is universal, spread over the whole world, that individual churches are only part of that church. It is not outside the visible, organized church that no one can have everlasting life, but it is outside the invisible body of Christ that we are denied everlasting life. Zwingli even went so far as to believe that church authority rests with the people but should be exercised by representatives. This, of course, is the Presbyterian form of government.

These truths were applied in a practical way to the Swiss people by the reformer. Many were the evils that needed reforming. When Zwingli first began to preach the truth Hoffman, one of the church authori-

Ulrich Zwingli and Switzerland   41

ties, said, "Suppose the priest should prove by witnesses what sins or what disorders had been committed by ecclesiastics in certain convents, streets, or taverns?" He and his colleagues then decided that Zwingli must be silenced. Chief of the evils needing reformation was immorality among the clergy. Marriage was forbidden the priests, but there were few who lived in the state of celibacy. They were required to behave not chastely but prudently. The pastor who competed with Zwingli for the call of the Zurich church was rejected partly for the reason that he was the father of six boys while supposedly a celibate. One incident should convince us of the conditions of the day. A married schoolmaster of Zurich, desiring to enter holy orders, obtained his wife's consent and with this view they separated. The new priest, finding it impossible to observe his vow of celibacy and unwilling to wound his wife's feelings, left the place where she lived and went to the See of Constance where he formed a criminal connection. His wife heard of this and followed him. The poor priest had compassion on her and, dismissing the woman who had usurped her rights, took his lawful wife into his house, but the procurator of the church immediately drew up a complaint. The vicar-general was in a ferment. The counselors of the consistory deliberated and ordered the curate either to forsake his wife or his benefice. The poor wife left her husband's house in tears and her rival re-entered it in triumph. The church declared itself satisfied, and from that time the adulterous priest was left undisturbed.

Money was another great evil. When Zwingli went to Zurich to be installed he was being addressed by the chief representative from the cathedral. He was charged, "You will make every exertion to collect the revenues of this chapter without overlooking the least. You will exhort the faithful both from the pulpit and in the confessional to pay all tithes and dues and to show by their offerings their affection for the church. You will be diligent in increasing the income arising from the sick, for masses and in general from every ecclesiastical ordinance." There was no charge except "money" given to Zwingli. Even the indulgence sellers rebuked the poor people that gathered around them, with the words, "Good folk, do not crowd so much. Make way for those who have money. We will afterward endeavor to satisfy those who have not."

Another great evil was ignorance. We have already said that in the disputations the Romans were always defeated because of their ignorance of the Bible and the fundamental truths of salvation. Before Zwingli came to Zurich, Fusslin, the poet and historian, said, "I have derived no instruction from the sermons of these priests." He and his intellectual friends ceased to attend. But Fusslin and Reuchlin, the treasurer of state, heard Zwingli's first sermon. Said they as they retired, "Glory be to God. This man is a preacher of the truth. He will be our Moses to lead us forth from this Egyptian darkness."

Yet another evil was that of idolatry. The people worshipped images, saints, and holy places. The image of the Virgin at Einsiedeln reputedly had the power of working miracles. Over the gate of the abbey could be read these words, "Here a plenary remission of sins may be obtained."

Mariolatry was another evil. While a boy studying at Berne under the Dominicans, Zwingli was saved from this. A young novitiate to the Dominican convent,

John Jetzer, was received at the same time. He was admitted on the sixth of January, 1507. On the first night a strange noise in his cell filled him with terror. The next night he was wakened by deep groaning. He saw a tall, white, sepulchral form standing by his bed. A voice said, "I am a soul escaped from the power of purgatory." Jetzer cried in alarm, "What can I do to save you?" The spector replied, "Scourge thyself eight days in succession until the blood comes and lie prostrate in the earth in the chapel of St. John." The novitiate submitted to the discipline and it was soon reported throughout the city that a soul had applied to the Dominicans in order to be delivered from purgatory. Great crowds came to the church to see the holy man who was prostrate on the pavement. Later the specter returned with two others and announced that Scotus, the inventor of the doctrine of the Immaculate Conception, was in purgatory. The appearances continued but one night when Mary was supposed to have appeared Jetzer fancied that he recognized the confessor's voice and on saying so out loud, Mary disappeared. Then she came again to censure the unbelieving brother. "This time it is the prior," exclaimed Jetzer, and rushed at him. Jetzer made his discovery public and as a result of the fraud four leaders of the convent perished at the stake. Such were the frauds constantly being practiced.

Against these, against the church's use of mercenaries, the selling of indulgences, the practice of abstinence during Lent, the use of confessions and penance and the belief in purgatory, Zwingli and his colleagues preached. Great success crowned their efforts in the emancipation of the people from superstition and error.

The reformers instituted changes immediately. First, they petitioned for the right of the clergy to marry, and a number of them, including Zwingli, without waiting for permission, proceeded to act upon their belief. They said that the Bible everywhere taught marriage and nowhere taught celibacy. They stressed the preaching of the Bible instead of the use of the mass and they urged the education of the people. They also instituted relief for the poor, who were to be clothed rather than the images. They even brought an end to the display of finery in public worship. These reformers were the forerunners of Puritanism, for the State legislated on the advice of the preachers, thereby controlling the moral life of the people.

Zwingli possessed certain weaknesses and errors. These we must not omit. In his youth he was drawn in with the spirit of the times to dissipation, but he utterly and completely freed himself from it through the power of the gospel and he became the exemplary head of a family. Zwingli erred in his identification of the church and the state. He did not fully grasp the principle which was later to develop through the Netherlands and the Separatists of England, of soul liberty, of authority by the state in civil matters only and in the church of spiritual matters only. Zwingli also erred in his sanction of the use of force. Well may Luther and Zwingli stand as examples for future generations on this matter. Luther declined the aid of temporal powers, rejected the force of arms, and looked for victory only in the profession of the truth. His efforts were crowned with the most brilliant success. Zwingli in turn sought help from the mighty ones of the earth, grasped the sword, and resorted to force. He witnessed a cruel and bloody catastrophe which ar-

Ulrich Zwingli and Switzerland

rested the progress of the Word of God in Switzerland. The Lord Himself has His own means of advancing the gospel and He does not commit His glory unto another.

III. THE UNIQUE TEACHING OF THE SWISS REFORM

There was a difference between the Lutheran and the Swiss Reformation. In order to understand this, we must think for a moment of the Roman doctrine of the mass, or of the holy eucharist. Rome believes and teaches that when the priest blesses the elements of bread and wine a miracle is performed and the substance is changed into the actual body and blood of Christ. This is called transubstantiation. In this theory, Christ is bodily present in the worship service of the mass. The people partake of the bread and the priests partake of the wine. The mass is the central sacrament and ceremony of the Roman Church. Everything else, such as penance, confession, and indulgences lead up to the mass. There the believer is in the Presence of God.

Luther did not completely break with Rome on this one matter. He taught that the words of Jesus in the sixth chapter of John, "This is my body," were literal. Luther believed that the resurrection body of Christ is ubiquitous, that is, everywhere present and thus present also in the wine and the bread. He believed that the resurrection body of Christ received supernatural attributes. This doctrine of Luther was called consubstantiation.

Zwingli's teaching states that the sacrament is only a memorial. He declared that the corporeal presence of Christ is an illusion. The words, "This is my body," actually mean, "This signifies my body," exactly as the verse in Exodus concerning the Passover, which says, "Ye shall eat it [the lamb] in haste: it is the Lord's passover," means it signifies the Lord's Passover, and as the words of Jesus concerning John the Baptist, "This is Elias," mean "This signifies Elias," for John denied that he was Elias. Zwingli proclaimed that the sacrament of the Lord's Supper merely represents the body and the blood of Christ and that the only presence is spiritual. Christ is present there as He is present in His church, pervading it, and the sacrament is a visible presentation of what Jesus has done for us. Zwingli feared lest the Christians, imagining that they had received Jesus Christ in the consecrated bread, should less earnestly seek to be united to Him by faith in the heart.

There came a time when at Marburg Luther and Zwingli met to discuss their differences. Luther took a very dogmatic attitude which had probably grown up from his controversies with many enemies. He was driven to his position by the extravagances of fanatics in Germany who by literalism rejected baptism, broke images, and pretended to inspiration. Therefore, in the controversy he clung tenaciously to this remnant of Romanism. Luther's principle in the Reformation was different from Zwingli's. Luther desired to maintain in the church all that is not expressly contrary to the Scriptures. Zwingli had a tendency to abolish all that cannot be proved by them. The former wished to remain united with the church of preceding ages, but to purify it. The latter passed over these ages and returned to the apostolic time, desiring the primitive condition of the church. Zwingli could not follow Luther. His more logical and rational thinking processes prevented him from accepting this Medievalism. The two, however, manifested the forbearance of love and the supreme principle of Protestantism, that there is unity in diversity and diversity in unity. They drew up a list of points on which they agreed. There were fourteen of them. On the fifteenth point they could not agree, so in this they first stated the matters of agreement and then in the last half point stated their diversities concerning the sacrament. This half of the fifteenth point is still the primary difference between sixty million Lutherans and all of those Protestants adhering to the reformed faith called "Presbyterians," "Congregationalists," "Episcopalians," and "Methodists."

We believe that Zwingli's position went beyond Luther's and is correct. We are convinced as was the monk who was listening to Zwingli's address in Berne on this subject preceding his celebration of the mass. He heard Zwingli quote from the Apostles' Creed, "He ascended into heaven and sitteth at the right hand of God the Father Almighty; from thence He shall come to judge the quick and the dead." Zwingli paused and then added, "These three articles are in contradiction to the mass." The priest stopped in astonishment at Zwingli's words. Then in the presence of the people who were electrified by the sermon he stripped off his priestly garments, threw them upon the altar, and exclaimed, "Unless the mass reposes on a more solid foundation I can celebrate it no longer." He became a convert to Protestantism.

We conclude then with the words of Jesus that it is the Spirit who quickeneth, the Holy Spirit who has been left here by Jesus to continue His work. Christianity is not a sacramental religion but a spiritual one. The Spirit calls us, regenerates us, and sanctifies us. It is the Spirit who quickens us by the memorial of the Lord's Supper so that it becomes a spiritual means of grace to our cleansing and consecration.

As long as the mass stands unattacked, Romanism is secure. As long as Romanism can lift up this sacrament called the "Host" and tell an ignorant people that it is Jesus Christ, it will continue in its power. Once reveal the error of that superstition and Romanism crumbles before the power of the Reformation.

Thus the Spirit and the bride say, "Come," and let all that are athirst come. Do not come to the communion of an organization with a visible head. Come to the communion of the only holy Catholic Church, which is the church universal, the body and the bride of Christ, redeemed by His precious blood shed once and for all as a sacrifice for the sins of those who believe.

JOHN CALVIN AND GENEVA
OR THE
TRUTH OF PREDESTINATION

III

JOHN CALVIN AND GENEVA
OR THE
TRUTH OF PREDESTINATION

"Whom he did foreknow, he also did predestinate to be conformed to the image of his Son, that he might be the first-born among many brethren. Moreover whom he did predestinate, them he also called: and whom he called, them he also justified: and whom he justified, them he also glorified."

THE city of Geneva, located at the southernmost tip of Lake Geneva where the Rhone river has its source, is second only to Paris in French cultural influence. The dominating figure of Geneva's history is John Calvin. A walk through the town quickly reveals that fact.

The modern city is divided by the southern point of the lake and the Rhone River. North of the lake, on the water front, runs the Quai du Mont Blanc, an avenue noted for its splendid view of the snow-capped Mont Blanc and surrounding peaks, for the beauty of its buildings and trees, and for its splendid hotels and consulates. Taking off from this avenue at an obtuse angle along the water's edge to the north is Quai du Wilson, ending at the palace of the nations, the magnificent new structure that will house the League in future days. Along this broad way is the Secretariat of the League, on the garden wall of which is an inscription to Woodrow Wilson, the idealist, who as President of the United States promulgated the idea of such a league during the war. Little did Wilson know when he dreamed of a league based upon an international covenant, having for its object the maintenance of peace by the development of co-operation between nations, that his own great nation would never take a part in it and that the embodiment of his ideal would some day become the partisan instrument of the dominating nations. Nevertheless, as one surveys the beautiful scene with his eyes, he cannot help but think with Wilson of what might have been.

The south of the lake, which is separated from the northern half of the city by the Rhone, and is connected by the Pont du Mont Blanc, comprises the old section of the town. In the center of the river is the Isle Rousseau with its prominent monument to the philosopher of nature whose theories embodied in the books, *Social Contract* and *Emile,* so powerfully influenced the French during the Revolution and became embodied in the American Declaration of Independence. On the south bank near the bridge is the national monument commemorating the entrance of this canton to the Swiss Confederation. Extending along the water front is the Lake Promenade, back of which is located that part of Geneva interesting to the student of history. From the fountain with a filmy jet rising two hundred and ninety-five feet high, south to the university, is the area formerly enclosed by the fortifications. Its center is the cathedral and around it are grouped the buildings connected with Calvin. First, there is the auditorium where Calvin and Knox preached in the sixteenth century. Next to it is the academy founded by Calvin and later developed into the great University of Geneva, with its famous library. Near by is the Rue Calvin, where Calvin lived during his exile, and the palace of justice, where the city officials ruled according to the Calvin constitution; and then in the center of the gardens facing the theater, the music conservatory, the electoral hall, the university, the Palace Enyard, and the museum of arts and history, is the Reformation monument built into the side of the hill. It is over one hundred yards long.

Standing before this gigantic monument one is impressed with the mighty influence of the spiritual and intellectual current that flowed out of this city in the sixteenth century and affected France, the Netherlands, Scotland, England, and America. That current had its source in the fountain of spiritual and intellectual life gathered around the four main figures on the monument. They are found in the center in high relief. First is Farel, then Calvin, then Beze, and then Knox. Each is depicted in his clerical robes, holding a Bible in his hand. Calvin's Bible is open, and he is standing a little forward from the group as though in the midst of an exposition of the Scripture, which was his constant practice during life. Farel was the forerunner of Calvin in Geneva; Beze was his colaborer at Geneva; and Knox received during the six years residence at Geneva with Calvin the inspiration for the Scotch-Protestant movement. In front of the pilasters on either side are statues of the political champions of the Reformation; to the left, Admiral Coligny, leader of the Huguenots, William of Orange, Stadtholder of the Netherlands, and Frederick the Great, elector of Brandenburg; to the right, Roger Williams, defender of the freedom of conscience in America, Oliver Cromwell, and Prince Stephen Bocskay of Transylvania. The bas-reliefs between the pilasters depict the history of Calvinism as it struggled against the blood and iron rule of Rome to bring liberty of conscience and worship to the peoples of Europe and America.

Concentrating on Calvin, we find from most pictures and descriptions of him that the most distinctive characteristic of his appearance was his eyes, which commanded respect, revealed the brilliance of intellect, and flashed with the power of indignation. His face was wan and a bit emaciated from long hours of study. His forehead was high, revealing the prominence of his thinking. His lips were firm, showing determination. His shoulders were a bit stooped, betraying the scholar. And his figure, though impressive, was not physically strong. At the age of sixteen, while Calvin was a leading student in the University of Paris, he commanded respect among his fellow students, which placed him even above the professors. At this time he was an ardent Catholic and even witnessed the burning of two Protestants at the stake before a slow fire in the presence of a huge multitude in front of the splendid cathedral of Notre Dame, that majestic symbol of Roman Catholicism. He was pursuing his studies for the priesthood, had already taken the tonsure, and was living on a benefice of the chaplaincy of his home town, Noyon, which was granted to him at the age of twelve.

Calvin had been born in the year 1509, just fifty-one miles northeast of Paris in Piccardy. His father was a clerk in the service of the church, and through influential contacts provided his son, who was a precocious youth, with the very best education. At the age of fourteen Calvin had finished two schools and commenced his studies in the University of Paris. These

John Calvin and Geneva

were interrupted, however, by a request from his father for him to take up law. He left Paris and devoted the energies of the next three years to mastering the principles of law in the University of Orleans. During these days he undermined his health, and found that he had no relish for the law. His real interest was in theology, and on the death of his father he returned to Paris to continue his classical studies. Sometime in this period at Paris he was suddenly converted through the instrumentality of certain professors who held Reformation doctrines. Because of his activity he was soon compelled to flee from Paris. While traveling in Switzerland he met Farel, who had won Geneva for the Reformation. After a few years of labor there, reaction set in and both these scholars were compelled to leave. Calvin settled in Strassburg, a city of refugees, where he entered upon a preaching ministry. After three years conditions were such in Geneva, because of riots and conflicts, that they begged Calvin to return. He did, and for the next twenty years of his life he labored in Geneva, establishing his educational system, formulating his political precepts, and courageously training the people in the Protestant truths.

The accomplishments of Calvin are amazing. Though suffering from ill health, he tenaciously continued his writing, which included the *Institutes of Religion*, the most profound and systematic statement of the Christian religion in the Protestant movement, nineteen commentaries on the Bible, laws, educational texts, refutations of Romanist teachings, and classical works. He preached constantly, even until his last sickness, when he had himself carried from his bed to his pulpit, and he became the leading influence in Protestant thought,

Calvin stopped with the theological movement of

Protestant dialectic. He was the dominant force in the civic life of Geneva, practically identifying the church with the state. When Calvin convicted Servetus of heresy, the state burned him at the stake. This position fell far short of what was to be the final Protestant position. In practice, Calvin denied the right of private judgment or the right of dissent. This was to be won by later Protestants, who carried the Reformation truths into political life. Calvin stood with Luther and Zwingli on all other great Protestant teachings, which were a reversion to the primitive church beliefs. On the matter of the sacraments he was Zwinglian, but he held to an Episcopal ministry. Zwingli and Luther were just as thorough believers in predestination as was Calvin. But because Calvin stated the teachings systematically, the Reformation truths have come to be known as Calvinism. Particular importance is placed upon predestination as the doctrine of Calvin because one Castellio rejected this truth and thereby drew attention to it.

Let us then examine briefly this one great doctrine that stands out in popular thinking as Calvinistic. There are in reality five main points of Calvinism. First, the truth of election, that God knows and establishes beforehand who shall belong to His redeemed people. Second, the truth of particular atonement, or that Christ died for those who should be saved. Third, the truth of total depravity, or that the human heart is essentially wicked due to the fall of the race. Fourth, the truth of irresistible grace; that the mysterious influence of the working of God's Spirit in the heart of the sinner cannot be resisted. And fifth, the truth of the perseverance of the saints; that those whom God had accepted in the Beloved shall neither totally nor finally fall away from the state of grace but shall persevere to the end and shall be eternally saved. This statement of the doctrine is a summary of the teaching of Paul, of Augustine, and of Calvin, although the first point, namely election, has most generally been connected with the name Calvin. We shall merely summarize the doctrines.

I. THE ESSENTIAL FACT OF FREEDOM

Though Calvin believed in election, he no less believed in freedom as an attribute of man. Freedom is a human intuition. Each of us is conscious of the ability to choose between two contrary objects, either of which he may will or perform. The idea of freedom is both negative and positive. A free man must be free from something and free for something. This does not mean that he is free in every realm. An American citizen is free within the limits of the laws of the state. He is free to go where he pleases and to do what he pleases. But he is not free from the physical laws which limit him. He cannot fly and he cannot be in two places at the same time. A man may think of any object which he chooses, but he is not free from the laws of thought. Human actions may be free from physical causality but they are not free from moral law. There is, in the words of a great philosopher, "the law of freedom."

We must distinguish between freedom and caprice. One does not chance to be what he is; he is largely governed by his past moral acts. But there is no causal necessity in these acts for him to transgress the law of God. There are two senses in which a man is free. When he is not a Christian he is free to do evil, and every choice has a downward tendency though his life may be moral. When he has been regenerated by the Spirit of God he is free to act in accordance with the law of God; although his deeds may not all be righteous, yet his trend is upward. Man is not free to transfer himself from one of these realms into another. This rests upon the sovereign grace of God. The prodigal son, while in his father's household, was free to order the servants around, to read from his father's library, to sit in the shade of the trees, and to enjoy his father's possessions. When he was in the far country he was free to feed swine and to work as a servant. He could not transfer himself from the realm of the swine to the realm of the family. He could make the contact through his will, but the transformation rested upon the act of the father. Just so we may place ourselves in a position to receive the regenerating power of God through the freedom of our will, but it is not our work that effects salvation.

This does not remove individual responsibility. The Bible specifically emphasizes this in connection with the fact of predestination. We read that "Judas by transgression fell, that he might go to his own place." Peter, in his Pentecostal sermon, announced concerning the crucifixion of Jesus, "Him, being delivered by the determinate counsel and foreknowledge of God, ye have taken and by wicked hands have crucified and slain." Paul was told by the angel while in the storm engulfing the ship, "There shall be no loss of any man's life among you, but of the ship." Yet when he saw the sailors abandoning the ship he said to the centurion and soldiers, "Except these abide in the ship, ye cannot be saved." Though God ordained safety, yet Paul knew that the skill and knowledge of the sailors were necessary to effect it. In each of these instances human freedom and Divine purpose are combined.

II. THE TRUTH OF PREDESTINATION

Predestination may be taken in the larger or in the smaller sense. In the larger it refers to the foreordination of everything that comes to pass. In this realm there must be a distinction between the efficient and the permissive decrees of God. All events which come to pass are embraced in the purpose of God, but they may come to pass by His own power or by His permitting their occurrence through the delegated free agencies of His creatures. That Satan would tempt the first pair of humanity to their fall and that a Saviour would come to save them from the results of the fall were equally embraced in the purposes of God. But the first was permitted and the second was decreed. God permitted Pharaoh to harden his heart. But Pharaoh did it. In the case of what God purposes to do, He is the agent, but never is He the author of sin. Nor does He limit the will of the creature. In the case of what He permits to be done, He is not the author and yet He has established the event. Hence, all things that come to pass are foreordained of God.

Predestination taken in its particular sense deals with the election to eternal life. God elects whom He will according to the good pleasure of His eternal purpose unto salvation. How large a body of the human family this is we have no means of knowing. He permits a number to be reprobate. The only logical basis for the salvation of children, especially those of unbelievers, is election. We know that infants dying within the covenant of a Christian family are redeemed and we postulate the mercies of the sovereign God to those dying out of the covenant. This same basis of God's sovereignty makes us hold out hope for moral heathen, such as Socrates, Marcus Aurelius, and Seneca. This was the position of Zwingli and of Calvin. It is only by a belief in predestination that we can hold this hope. Otherwise we must thoroughly reject the Bible teaching about sin and salvation. Thinking of the concept of justice, we must observe that all of us, being evil, from the results of our own transgressions and from the imputation of sin through the progenitor and representative of the human race, are worthy of condemnation. It is only by the mercy of Almighty God that any of us are saved.

Do not confuse predestination with fatalism. The only similarity of the two beliefs concerns the certainty of events. Fatalism denies a supreme intelligence and relegates the certainty of events to causal necessity. It loses the purposive development which is stated in predestination whereby all things are declared to work together for good. The truth of predestination states that the events are determined by infinite wisdom and goodness. Fatalism believes that the moral actions of rational agents are as much determined as are physical actions, whereas predestination proclaims the freedom and responsibility of man for his moral action. Herein is the difference between a man and a machine. Fatalism denies moral distinctions and leads to despair, whereas predestination makes qualitative distinctions and leads to hope.

For a clear illustration of fatalism read that heartrending story of Thamilla, by Ferdinand Duchene, a former French judge in Algiers. Out of his experience, with ample justification of every event which he weaves into the story, he makes the lovely character Thamilla move through harrowing experiences of life, resigning herself because of her belief in fate. Fatalism utterly controlled the thinking of all who forced this turtledove of Algiers through her suffering. Such a view is renounced by Calvinism and the Bible.

The belief in predestination does not destroy the motive for further sanctification in the Christian life. God ordains the means as well as the end. If He purposes that a man live, He purposes that he should also eat. If He purposes that he should be holy, He also determines that he should pray. Psychologically, it is true that the stronger the hope of success is in the individual, the greater will be his motive to exertion toward the end purposed.

III. The Harmony of Predestination and Freedom

We can never work out a complete reconciliation between these two truths in the limited human mind. We must continue to look on two sides of every question, the Divine side and the human side. If we look on any act from the standpoint of God, we realize that He foreknew it before it came to pass, and therefore it had to be established. If we look at it from the human side we realize that nobody knew that it was to come to pass and therefore it was uncertain. As limited human beings we cannot predict the moral acts of a free agent though we can make some predictions of physical necessity on the basis of scientific hypothesis.

Since man does not know what is predestined and foreordained, it becomes his challenge to rise above his background of heritage, his environment, and his past experience, and to strike out on a moral conquest for his soul. Thereby, he intuitively knows that he is responsible for choices that he makes.

Anyone who has the conception of God as infinite believes in His omniscience. Whatsoever God knows God must also have established. Therefore, even to admit the existence of the Almighty makes us admit the fundamental principle underlying predestination. No difficulty is as great as that of accounting for this world and the life of a man without God. With the truth of God, the difficulties attendant on the belief in predestination are minor. They need not overthrow our faith. The Bible tells us of an almighty and infinite God. It also teaches the truth of predestination. The belief in this God enables us to believe in His works in the world.

The man who in humble resignation will commit his way unto the God of the Bible is in safety. This God invites us to come to Him for salvation. His Word says, "Whosoever will believe on the Lord Jesus Christ shall be saved." The way is open for those who will believe, to believe. Christ has died for His people and through faith in His finished work we are saved by grace. Whether we will believe or not believe morally but not metaphysically, depends on us. Jesus said, "Him that cometh to Me I will in no wise cast out," and "He that will do the will of God shall know the doctrine." If then we conform ourselves to the revealed will of God, nothing can separate us from His love. "There is now no condemnation to them who are in Christ Jesus."

This truth was the great incentive to the accomplishments of John Calvin. It was his comfort in his struggles and suffering. It inspired his faith to face great obstacles. It was the power that sustained men in their defeats in the Reformation struggle. It is a foundation of the Christian faith.

WILLIAM OF ORANGE AND THE NETHERLANDS
OR
CHRISTIAN LIBERTY

IV

WILLIAM OF ORANGE AND THE NETHERLANDS
OR
CHRISTIAN LIBERTY

"Render unto Caesar the things which are Caesar's and unto God the things that are God's."

THE teaching of this text was first put into practice by William of Orange, fifteen hundred years after it had been stated by Jesus Christ. William of Orange symbolizes all that is precious to the Netherlanders. Like Washington, he is the father of his country. But Orange has a broader and deeper meaning to the world, and especially to the Americans, than the patriotic part he played in the Dutch wars for civil liberty. It was William of Orange who broke the power of the Spanish Inquisition and who gave to the world the principle, not of religious tolerance, but of religious liberty. He completely grasped and espoused a principle of freedom which even the Protestant princes of Germany and of Switzerland failed to apprehend.

William of Orange began where Luther left off in the great Reformation. Luther had contended for the principle of justification by faith, the authority of the Scriptures, and the individual right to interpret those Scriptures. These three principles spread widely through Europe in the religious phase of the Reformation. But the great battle for the political right to live according to these principles was not fought in Luther's day.

Luther was enabled to do his great work because he was protected by Frederick, Elector of Saxony, who along with other princes of the German provinces, was able to defy the emperor. Zwingli and Calvin were able to carry on their religious teaching in Switzerland because the Swiss cantons were free from the domination of the empire and from kings. Each city was sovereign and was united to the other cities of the Swiss confederation. The only military interference with the liberties of the Swiss cantons came from other cantons of the confederation that did not espouse the Reformation. It was left for the Netherlands to work out the principles of religious liberty.

Reformation truths were quickly accepted in the Netherlands. The great Erasmus was a Dutchman. The Brethren of the Common Lot had their headquarters in the Netherlands. The Bible was translated into the Dutch, and the predominant influence in the beginning was Lutheran, although gradually the Calvinists came to be stronger. At the same time the French Reformation was gaining ground, and though persecution raged against it under Francis I, and later under Catherine de Medici, the numbers of converts increased and many churches existed secretly.

In the middle of the sixteenth century events took a new turn. The Emperor Charles V was compelled by the German princes at the Peace of Augsburg to grant them the privilege of choosing the religion for their provinces. This did not amount to religious liberty, for Catholics were not permitted true liberty in Protestant provinces, nor were the Protestants granted liberty in the Catholic provinces. In 1555 the "Peace of Religion" was signed, in which the emperor agreed not to persecute any for his religious beliefs. Had

William of Orange and The Netherlands 67

this been adhered to the history of Europe would have been different. But Charles was still under the influence of the pope, and when he abdicated in favor of his son Philip in the next year, he urged him to exterminate heresy. Philip immediately revived the edicts of persecution in the Netherlands, revised the government so that it would be under his immediate control, and initiated a series of murders that in a few years reached the amazing toll of sixty thousand. The conception that motivated Philip and was inspired by Pius IV was, "extermination of heresy by exterminating the heretics." Into this scene came William of Orange.

I. THE LIFE OF WILLIAM OF ORANGE

William, prince of Orange, was born of a noble Roman Catholic family whose ancestry went back to the beginnings of Netherland history. In marriage his father and mother had united the two provinces of Nassau and Orange, which were the wealthiest sections of the most prosperous north countries. The father of William ranked high in the service of the emperor. He was a personal friend of Charles V and died at his feet in the aftermath of a great battle. The emperor was so indebted to the Prince of Orange for service and support that he took his son William at the age of ten into his court as a page. It seems that the child was beautiful and precocious and became the favorite of the nobles. He sat in all of the councils that determined the great movements in Europe. He learned how wars were begun and settled, how ambitions and intrigue governed the affairs of nations, and he saw the deceitfulness and the power that rested in the hands of the clergy. It was a splendid training for the future part he was to play in history. As Charles grew older he leaned more and more on the youthful William of Orange. In fact, William assisted him to his feet when he read his speeches, and was his constant companion through a number of years. He knew the duplicity of the king in signing the "Peace of Religion" and yet in urging his son Philip to promote the persecution of heresy. When Charles was ready to abdicate, the result of his many campaigns of war in Germany, France, Spain, and Austria were returning upon his head. With a sense of failure he turned over the reins of government to Philip at a great celebration in the Netherlands. And then he retired to a monastery in Spain.

William was present at the crowning of Philip, and he took a prominent part in what is called the "Joyous Entry" of Philip into the Netherlands. People had great hope that Philip would now grant true toleration to the Protestants. Great festivals were held in Brussels and Antwerp. Oxen were roasted in streets, and the people rejoiced. But the new king quartered a large Spanish army on the people and immediately declared the edicts of persecution in operation in violation of their charters and demanded a large appropriation from the people. A few years before this time William had been hunting in France with the Duke of Alva, King Henry of France, and others. During the chase Henry took William aside and confided to him that a plot existed between himself and Philip and Pope Pius to establish the Inquisition in the Netherlands and there to crush heresy. William was horror-struck with the details of the plot, which included plans to murder tens of thousands of his own countrymen by the most cruel methods. From that moment, at the age of twenty-three, he determined that every effort

William of Orange and The Netherlands 69

of his life would go toward freeing his countrymen from the Inquisition. But William confided nothing of his plans to others and came to be known as William the Silent. While still in the graces of the king he organized a system of espionage so that the private letters of Philip were copied every night and immediately forwarded to him. Through this, during the next twenty years, he was able to anticipate every move of the Emperor and of his emissaries.

At the accession of Philip, William began systematically to oppose each of his moves to bring about the organization and machinery necessary for the Inquisition. At the end of four years Philip left the Netherlands because of the mounting hatred of the people and as he was about to depart he turned to William, who had been his personal host, and said, "Not the Estates have opposed me, but you, you, you." William had scored his first victory in removing Philip but in his place was left the Bishop of Aaras and regent, Margaret of Parma. These continued the persecution of the Protestants. Gradually, Orange succeeded in bringing pressure to bear for the removal of the Spanish troops. Already, however, the country had been divided into bishoprics and archbishoprics, and over the archbishops a cardinal, Granvelle, who was a cruel, arrogant man, exercising the absolute power of a monarch. Twenty inquisitors came from Spain, and now the persecution began in earnest.

No one can read of the Inquisition without mingled amazement and horror. It was commenced as an instrument against the Jews and the Moors, but it was gradually turned against the Protestants. From the pope the control had passed to the hands of Torquimada, a Dominican friar. In eighteen years he destroyed one hundred and fourteen thousand families for no crime whatever. The accused victims, whether men, women, or tender virgins, were stripped naked and fastened to a wooden bench and with water, weights, fires, pulleys, and screws, their bodies were tortured the longest possible time without causing death in order that confession might be made. When confession was made the victims were burned, and if not made, they were burned for obstinacy. One illustration will suffice to show the cruelties of this regime. A man, Le Blas, had denounced a priest for erroneous preaching concerning the sacrament. For this offense he was thrice put to the torture, then dragged to the market-place, where his right hand and foot were burned and twisted off between two hot irons, his tongue was torn out by the roots, and with his arms and legs fastened together behind him, he was hung by an iron chain hooked to his back and swung to and fro over a slow fire until he was entirely roasted. In Spain these burnings, called "Auto-de-fes," were occasions of great recreation to the inquisitors and their friends. They were preceded by groups of school children, followed by magistrates and nobility, and attended by harangues and chants. It was this that William vowed to keep from his people.

Nevertheless, the day came when one of the parties to the conspiracy, the Duke of Alva, arrived in the Netherlands with thousands of Spanish troops. He immediately set up the Inquisition and in a short time had tortured eighteen thousand. Tens of thousands of the Dutch people fled to England; others to the woods. Commerce stopped, mourning was general, and the cities fell into despair. At this time William of Orange embraced the Protestant religion. He had hitherto been a Roman Catholic, obedient to the emperor, refusing to support the Reformation movements. But now he made his choice. Through a study of the Bible he came to the Protestant conclusions, and though religion was not the primary factor in his life, he now became the recognized leader of the Reformation armies. Co-operating with him were Count Coligny, of France, with his Huguenots, Prince Maurice, of Saxony, with his Germans, and many Catholics of the Netherlands. The Prince of Orange married Anna, daughter of Maurice, of Saxony, and now began to gather troops to oppose the terrors being perpetrated in the Netherlands.

II. THE WARS OF LIBERTY

The followers of Prince William were called the "Beggars." In the early days of the persecutions, before war was thought of, the lesser princes of the Netherlands, Catholics, Lutherans and Protestant, signed a petition which was submitted to the Regent Margaret, requesting the cessation of persecution. When the petition was presented to the council by Brederode, Cardinal Granvelle said, "Who are these beggars?" From this statement, an organization was formed called "Beggars" and it later became the nucleus of the army that opposed the Spaniards. At the same time great preaching services were held in the Netherlands. Huge rewards were placed on the heads of the preachers by the government, but the people gathered in great multitudes of ten to twenty thousand outside the cities and listened to these preachers. No native troops could be obtained to arrest them for they went to hear the preachers themselves.

The importation of the Spanish troops enabled the Regent to enforce the laws against religion. Four of the six counts, including Edgemont, were seized and killed, and William of Orange declared war against the Spanish regent, gathered an army, and began the attack. The succeeding war lasted through many years and was attended with successes and failures. At its beginning the French support was withdrawn because Catherine, the queen mother of Charles IX of France, perpetrated the massacre of St. Bartholmew's Day, which claimed the lives of nearly seventy thousand Huguenots. The French Protestants had to defend themselves.

This massacre is one of the horrible stories in history. The principal Protestants were invited to Paris under a solemn oath of safety to celebrate the marriage of the King of Navarre, a Protestant, with the daughter of the French king. The marriage was an attempt at a compromise solution of the religious question which had caused wars to follow one another in quick succession. Admiral Coligny was the leader of the Huguenot forces. While the negotiations were in progress over the marriage, which was to unite the two parties and give peace to France, Coligny was invited to the court and enjoyed repeated interviews with the youthful King Charles IX. He urged the king to join forces with the Netherlands against Spain. While the king wavered, Catherine, the queen mother, used all of her powers on her son Charles to prevent his conversion to the Protestant view. Then in conjunction with the Duke of Guise, she plotted the massacre of all the Protestants, beginning with the nobility to be assembled in Paris for the wedding and extending to the provinces. In some way by appealing to the fears and suspicions of the king, Catherine prevailed on him to give the fatal decree. Plans were quickly executed

William of Orange and The Netherlands 73

and by dawn the next morning, August 24, 1572, the massacre began. First the Catholic forces went to the hotel of Admiral Coligny, where the guard became accomplices of the murderers. Swift work was made of him, following which in a systematic way the Catholic population of Paris was raised against the Huguenots with the cry, "Kill, kill!" The day became a carnival of blood in which ten thousand were slain in Paris and thousands more in the provinces. The strength of Protestantism in France was broken and her leaders dead. When the pope received the news at Rome, he declared a universal jubilee, had coins struck off with his image on one side and on the other a rude representation of the massacre with an angel brandishing a sword. Perefixe, a Roman historian, estimates that one hundred thousand perished in the massacre.

The high points of the war for Dutch liberty consisted of the successes of the Dutch on the water, where ships, operating with Letters of Marque granted by Prince William, preyed constantly upon the Spanish, and were completely victorious upon the sea. The Dutchmen proved themselves to be fearless fighters. Time and again a few small ships defeated large numbers of Spanish galleons. At one time the Spanish forces laid siege to the city of Leyden. The inhabitants were in desperate straits and relief could in no way be brought to them, but they held out for over four months. The Dutch cut the dykes and gradually the sea waters inundated the land and the Dutch fleet sailed in over the tops of the trees and brought relief to the starving people. The victory was celebrated by the founding of the University of Leyden. At the close of the wars the country was divided. The Catholic provinces became what is now known as Belgium. Seven northern provinces entered the Union of Utrecht and became known as the United Provinces of Netherlands. These were Protestant and permitted absolute freedom of religion.

III. THE INFLUENCE OF WILLIAM OF ORANGE

William was spared long enough to complete his work. Philip had placed a price on his head of twenty-five thousand gold crowns and elevation to the rank of nobility to the family of the assassin. Numerous attacks were made upon the life of William without success, until finally a Catholic of Burgundy, named Gerard, posed as a Protestant refugee and gradually became a trusted minister of the Prince of Orange. One day while conferring with the Prince for a passport he whipped out a pistol which he had purchased with the Prince's own money and shot him. The Prince's last words were, "God have mercy on my people." And as his sister asked him if he trusted Christ, the Captain of his salvation, he answered, "Yes," and expired.

The principle for which William contended was separation of the church and the state by which complete religious liberty for all should be entertained. William was as much opposed to Protestant domination of the state as he was to Roman domination of the state. Upon this principle the Netherlands became a haven for refugees from all parts of Europe. For this reason it became the dwelling place of the pilgrims who faced the same kind of persecution in England that the Huguenots had met in France and the Calvinists had met in the Netherlands under the Roman rule. These pilgrims later went to America and the principle of religious liberty was planted in Plymouth and

William of Orange and The Netherlands 75

reached its climax in the statement of Roger Williams, who founded Rhode Island, that "the province of the magistrate is confined to civil things only." In this the Reformation was complete. William of Orange founded the Dutch Republic on the doctrine of freedom for all in matters of religion. Washington fought for the same principle when he used his personal influence to induce the framers of the Constitution of the United States to adopt the following amendment, "Congress shall make no law respecting the establishment of religion, or prohibiting the free exercise thereof."

When England passed through its great struggle with the house of James II, it invited William III, Prince of Orange, to become king of England. He was a descendant of William, Prince of Orange, of Coligny, the great Huguenot, and of Charles I of England. He succeeded in driving the Catholic Stuarts from England and by what is known as "The Glorious Revolution" the succession of Protestant sovereigns was established on the British throne. Until the English people will it, no Catholic potentate can ever wear Britain's diadem. This was the work of William III, Prince of Orange.

Ireland remained Catholic, and James II attempted to repair his fortunes with the help of French troops by landing in Ireland and making it the base of operations against England. In a short time the armies of James and the Orangemen of William met at the battle of Boyne. William's Orangemen were completely victorious, and the whole country submitted to William III.

From this it is easy to see why the feeling against Orangemen, celebrating the Battle of Boyne on July 12, is still manifested. "In the light of history it means: William of Orange, or Philip of Spain? It means: Reformation, or Inquisition? It means: perfect religious liberty or cruel priestly tyranny. It means: Christ or the pope. It means: the Prince of Orange or St. Patrick. It means: America for all or America for Catholics only. It means: a free Bible or the Council of Trent. It means: Freedom or despotism." It means: Peace on earth and good-will to men or the extermination of heresy by exterminating heretics.

The principle of "Render unto Caesar the things that are Caesar's and unto God the things that are God's," or the principle of religious liberty is a basic principle of American idealism, and we received it through the instrumentality of the Reformation and in particular the Prince of Orange. What others have died to bequeath to us as a priceless heritage, let us not despise. Let the motto of the house of Orange be our motto: "I will maintain."

JOHN KNOX AND SCOTLAND
OR
THE POWER OF CONSCIENCE

V

JOHN KNOX AND SCOTLAND
OR
THE POWER OF CONSCIENCE

"How much more shall the blood of Christ, who through the eternal Spirit offered himself without spot to God, purge your conscience from dead works to serve the living God?"

JOHN KNOX can only be understood in his native setting—Bonnie Scotland. Of the few countries besides our own that we learn to love, Scotland is one. It is unique in its beauty—the rugged hills, the quiet lakes, the rapid rivers, the sentinel-like, centuries-old castles, surrounded with legends and ever clothed in mystery. Scotland makes a perennial appeal to the traveler and dreamer. There is romance in that country—the romance of the clans, of the feuds, of great fighters, of murders, of loyalties, of love of liberty, and of men that are men. Who does not wish to visit Ayr and dream of Robby Burns, or Abbotsford on the Tweed and relive the life of Scotland as seen by Sir Walter Scott, or Stirling Castle and remember Rob Roy and Robert the Bruce! There is religion in Scotland, and it runs deep. The people have produced great preachers, theologians, and philosophers. They are stern religionists, making austere demands, but producing character which is second to none. Little wonder that Scotland was fertile soil for the great principles of the Reformation.

Sometimes we have wondered why it is that the little countries are peopled by men who are able to inspire the world. Two of the smallest were Greece and the Netherlands, and both in ancient and in modern history have been unexcelled in their contributions to art, sculpture, science, and philosophy. We need only mention names such as Leibnitz, Spinoza, Rubens, Rembrandt, Van Eck, Van Dyke, Van Loon, and the four Nobel prize-holders now resident at the University of Leyden to substantiate this statement for the Netherlands. No one needs to have called to his attention the great names of antiquity: Phidias, Solon, Lycurgus, Aristotle, Socrates, Pericles, and others. Similarly, the two countries, Scotland and Switzerland, make a contribution at present to the emotional and aesthetic life of cosmopolitan citizens. Few there be who ever travel who do not grow attached to these little countries, but great peoples.

John Knox was a typical Scot. Commonly, we are shown portraits of Knox, both by word and pen, that are caricatures. Most people have the picture of a stern, glaring old man with a long beard, who with cutting, hard words lashed into submission a young and beautiful queen and a submissive people. But this is not the true picture of Knox. Thomas Carlyle examined all extant portraits of his time and then attempted to draw the true portrait of Knox. The result was a fearless, honest, rugged but blunt Scotchman, embodying the good characteristics of his people. He was a diligent student, possessed of sharp intellectual discernment, power of expression, depth of conviction, and an honest, burning zeal, and he was a man of genius, "a heaven-inspired seer, a heroic leader of men." The outstanding trait of Knox's character was the predominance of his conscience. When the Queen attempted to entrap Knox by elevating him to the position of her private adviser outside of the times of his public preaching, he said, "Neither my conscience nor my office will permit me to do this." At another time he pleaded with her not to reject the mercy of God but to make her peace with Him. She answered, "My conscience is not disturbed and is quite content to live and die with the Romanists." Said Knox, "Conscience, madam, requires knowledge. I fear me that the right knowledge ye have not. The Bible is the teacher of conscience." In the midst of his titanic struggle thoroughly to free Scotland from the power of Rome, Knox was once preaching in the cathedral of St. Giles before the nobility. In the midst of his discourse upon the providences of God within the realm, he referred to his previous admonitions and then addressed the nobles directly, "Ask your consciences and let them answer you before God, if I—not I, but God's Spirit by me—in your greatest extremities willed you not ever to depend upon your God." As usual, it was a direct appeal to the conscience. In Knox's last interview with Queen Mary before he was tried and acquitted for treason at her instigation, he was quietly reproving her for her actions when she burst into a fit of weeping and a flood of tears. While courtiers attempted to calm her, Knox stood still without any alteration of countenance for a long season until the Queen was pacified. Then he said, "Madam, in God's presence I speak. I never delighted in the weeping of any of God's creatures, yea, I can scarcely well abide the tears of my own boys whom my own hand correcteth; much less can I rejoice in Your Majesty's weeping. But, seeing I have offered to you no just occasion to

82   *Our Protestant Heritage*

be offended, but have spoken the truth as my vocation craves of me, I must sustain, albeit unwillingly, Your Majesty's tears, rather than I dare hurt my conscience, or betray my commonwealth through my silence." Knox was a man under the power of conscience.

I. THE REFORMERS AND KNOX

We are not to think that John Knox was the first leader of the Reformation in Scotland. While he was yet a young man, a student of noble blood, by name Patrick Hamilton, came fresh from the universities of Europe, filled with the teaching of Luther and began so to preach, and in the space of one month he was burned by Archbishop James Beaton at the castle of St. Andrews. Soon after, George Wishart embraced the Protestant teachings. He was driven out of Scotland, sought refuge at Cambridge University in England, and later when certain Scottish Lords promised him protection, returned to that land. He began immediately to preach at East Lothian and Haddington, where John Knox was tutor to the sons of the Lord of Langniddry. Here this young priest, steeped in the knowledge of the classics and of the lore of the church, came into contact with the Reformed doctrine. Soon Beaton, now a cardinal, attempted to apprehend Wishart, and Knox was a constant companion of Wishart as he traveled about preaching and escaping the assassin of the cardinal. Finally, Bothwell, later the third husband of Mary of Scotland, apprehended Wishart and he was taken to St. Andrews a prisoner, where he was burned at the stake.

About this time, Knox was thoroughly converted. It came about through his reading the fourteenth chapter of John. He had already been a priest for sixteen years, living after the common mode. In speaking of it, Knox said, "It was the fourteenth of John that first spoke to my heart. Here, thought I, is what I require, and I seized upon the divine word with the joy and appreciation of a starving man. When the heart feels itself lost and aching, it delights in the very syllables of the Scripture." Following this, Knox thought he was alone, without helper or friend, and found his entire consolation in the Scripture while he taught in the family of Hugh Douglas in East Lothian. Cardinal Beaton then set about to take Knox, but he himself was set upon by some armed men and slain. They were converts to the doctrine of Wishart. They seized the castle of St. Andrews, and now that the pupils of Knox took refuge in St. Andrews, he followed them and became identified with the beginnings of this movement.

The castle of St. Andrews still stands overlooking St. Andrews Bay, famous in Scottish history. Though in ruins it is still pointed out with its great dungeon where religious prisoners were kept. While living in the castle, Knox was strangely called to preach. It was the custom for the people to select the man whom they considered God had endowed with the power of preaching. While in the cathedral of St. Andrews, the minister, John Rough, was expounding the Scriptures when suddenly he turned toward Knox and said in the hearing of all, "Brother, ye do ill to neglect the call of God. Ye are endowed with gifts which the church requires, and I charge ye not to tarry but to take up the work of preaching and laboring in the pastor's office." Knox records the incident in his history of the Scottish Reformation. He said, "As I sat confused he turned to the congregation saying, 'Did ye not so charge me and do I not this by your commandment?' It thrilled my heart like to rending to hear the strong-armed men and gentle women reply, 'Yea, it is our call.' I left the kirk in sore agony of mind. But after long prayer I obeyed the voice of God and began to preach in the congregation." Knox immediately became the outstanding preacher of the Reformed group.

The next year a French fleet appeared before St. Andrews in answer to the plea from the Queen Regent, Mary Guise of Lorraine, and the city and castle were taken from the Protestants. The leaders were taken to France; the lords were placed in prison, and John Knox was sent to the galleys. Not only was this important in the history of the Reformation but it was important in the history of Scotland, for as a reward, the French took back with them the little Mary Stuart, later to be Mary, queen of Scots. At five years of age she was thus sent to France to be betrothed to the dauphin (Francis II) son of Catherine de Medici and Henry II. In the galleys, Knox suffered for nineteen months, and in the court of France the child Mary was inculcated not only with the culture and learning of the day, but also with the arrogance and the wickedness of Catherine de Medici.

At the end of the nineteen-month period, in a battle with the English fleet, the galley on which Knox served was captured, and he was freed. For five years under Edward VI, son of Henry VIII, he labored as one of the leaders of the English Reformation as chaplain to the King. Twice he was offered a bishopric and twice he declined because he did not feel that the English church was as yet sufficiently reformed. But as a mighty power in preaching, he stirred up the people to good works, he put an end to rioting, and he was the main spokesman before the English council. But suddenly Edward died and Bloody Mary, the daughter of Henry VIII and Catherine of Aragon, came to the throne. Then began the fires of Smithfield when the martyrdoms commenced. Ridley, Latimer, and later Cranmer were burned at Oxford. Protestants fled from England, and one of the last to go was Knox, making his retreat through France to Geneva, where Calvin was at the head of the government and church. Here he remained for four years in close communion with the greatest thinker the church has produced since the days of Augustine until he was invited to return to Scotland by the Protestant lords who had succeeded in seizing sufficient power to guarantee his safety. Meanwhile, Mary of Scotland became the Queen of France as the wife of Francis II.

Knox returned to his native land and joined with the lords of the congregation in a war against the queen regent, Mary Guise of Lorraine, and her Frenchmen. Town after town armed in favor of Knox and his cause; the population arose and with the help of Elizabeth of England drove out the French. Then followed the organization of the Scottish Reformed Church, when the Protestant principles entered into full power. Not without significance in these wars was what is called the Covenant. The first one was signed by the lords of the congregation who agreed to lay down their lives, property, and future hopes for the sake of ridding themselves of the enemies of Christ and for the propagation of the Word of God. Thereinafter such Presbyterians were called Covenanters because they covenanted at the cost of all to abide by the Reformed truth.

II. THE WOMEN AND KNOX

While still in France and Geneva, Knox wrote a book entitled, *The First Blast of the Trumpet Against the Monstrous Regiment of Women.* It came at a time when women were on many of the thrones of Europe. It was primarily instigated by the excesses of Mary Tudor, Queen of England, and wife of Emperor Philip II, who was promoting the Inquisition in the Netherlands. Secondarily, it was directed against Mary Guise of Lorraine, a Frenchwoman who was the delegated regent of Scotland, against Margaret of Parma who was Queen Regent of the Netherlands during the Inquisition, and against Catherine de Medici, who was the Queen Mother in France. This last woman is suspected of murdering her own son Francis that she might have the throne of France, is accused of so completely degrading her children in debauchery that she could control Charles IX, her second son, King of France, and it has been proved that she was the chief instigator of the Massacre of St. Bartholomew's Day in conjunction with the brother of the Queen Regent of Scotland, the Duke of Guise. It is typical of Knox that he should speak out against this monstrous regiment of women who were cursing Europe with blood and slaughter. And yet it is to be regretted that this of all the works of Knox is the one most relied upon as the source of literary opinion as to his character. Even Calvin thought Knox was a bit hard on the women and remonstrated with him concerning this blast. The most regrettable part of it was that though it was primarily written against Mary Tudor, it was not published until Elizabeth became Queen of England. She was a Protestant and ended the persecution. Elizabeth never forgave

John Knox and Scotland

Knox for this treatise, and the blast also became a source of the differences between the beautiful Mary, Queen of Scots, and Knox in their later years. In the midst of these facts which sometimes have brought the name of Knox into disrepute, it is helpful to read the conclusion of Carlyle. He said, "One ought to add withal that Knox was no despiser of women; far the reverse in fact; his behaviour to good and pious women is full of respect, and his tenderness, his patient helpfulness in their suffering and infirmities are beautifully conspicuous."

Much has been written about Knox and Mary, Queen of Scots. This relationship has been used oftener to defame the reformer and to bring reproach upon the early Presbyterian movement than almost anything else. Perhaps a word ought to be said. Mary was both a pitiable and an admirable personality. She was one of the most learned, cultured, and well read women of her day, as well as noted for her beauty. It was her custom to have important books read to her after her evening meal. She was a leader of her generation. She is to be pitied because of her tragic life, which was partly a victim of circumstance. It was not her fault that she was taken to France and kept under the influence of the Guise family and the hated cardinal of Lorraine. As she said to Knox, no one had dared to oppose her will in France, and she expected the same in Scotland. She is not responsible for her beauty, which involved her in trouble, or for the fact that she was a Romanist when her own people were turning to the Reformation. On the other hand, there are matters of responsibility in connection with Mary. She showed that she was governed by emotion when she married Lord Darnley. And she descended to moral depths when she married Lord Bothwell, the murderer of Darnley. Moreover, she was largely responsible for her own imprisonment under Elizabeth when she put forth the claims of her son James to the English throne. In Mary, Queen of Scots, we see the mingling of one's choices with one's environment and heritage. And her life was a tragedy because it was lived on a stage set for the titanic struggle between Romanism and the Reformers.

Some say that Knox was too rough and hard to Queen Mary. Hear the word of Carlyle on this subject: "Knox's conduct to Queen Mary, the harsh visits he used to make in her own palace, to reprove her there, have been much commented upon. Such cruelty, such coarseness, fills us with indignation! On reading the actual narrative of the business, what Knox said and what Knox meant, I must say, one's tragic feeling is rather disappointed. They are not so coarse, these speeches; they seem to me about as fine as the circumstances would permit. Whoever reading these colloquies thinks they are vulgar insolences of a plebeian priest to a delicate, high lady, mistakes the purport and essence of them altogether. It was, unfortunately, not possible to be polite to the Queen of Scots, unless one proved untrue to the nation and cause of Scotland. A man who did not wish to see the land of his birth made a hunting field for intriguing, ambitious Guises, and the cause of God trampled under foot of falsehoods, formulas, and the devil's cause, had no method of making himself agreeable. The hapless queen!—but the still more hapless country, if she were made happy!"

This does not conclude Knox's relationship with women, however. He successfully courted the daughter of Robert Bowes, a Romanist, and married her after she and her mother had embraced the Reformation. She was a beautiful and faithful wife with whom he lived tenderly until her death when he was fifty-six years of age. At the age of fifty-nine, in the midst of his great triumph and most widespread influence, Knox married Margaret Stuart, of royal blood. At this Queen Mary stormed. Two sons were born by his first wife and three daughters by his last wife. Both unions were happy and blessed.

III. KNOX AND PRESBYTERIANISM

In September, 1772, couriers brought the news about the fearful Massacre of St. Bartholomew's Day. Before the horror that seized the city had diminished, fresh details came by successive posts, until Scotland was in a frenzy of anger and horror. "Carry me to my pulpit," said Knox, and they did so. With a mighty effort, he summoned all his little strength and denounced the vengeance of God upon the wicked king Charles and Queen Mother who had committed this foul wrong. Said he in tones that long lived in the memory of his hearers, "Let the French ambassador tell his master that sentence is pronounced against him in Scotland. Let him say to the king of France that vengeance shall never part from his house unless he repent. Tell ye this persecutor that his name shall descend to all time as a scorn and reproach and none of his race shall possess the kingdom in peace." The ambassador quitted the kingdom in a rage.

The great characteristic of Knox's preaching was his fearlessness and his outspokenness. As a citizen he was subject to the laws of the state and the will of his sovereign. In his pulpit he was subject only to the will of God. He spoke that will without fear or favor.

Hardened soldiers listened to him in awe. Queens, regents, and lords trembled. Mary is reported to have said, "I fear the prayers of John Knox more than the armies of England." Knox stirred the lords of the congregation to their courageous action by his preaching and he went with them to the battlefields. There was a sincerity of spiritual life about him, illustrated by the fact that he was overheard in the narrow enclosure in the rear of his residence on High Street, Edinburgh, praying, "O Lord, give me Scotland or I die." There was a power about his ministry which was dynamic. "Here more than elsewhere Knox proves himself the Hebrew prophet in complete perfection; he refuses to soften any expression or to call anything by its milder name, or in short, for a moment to forget that the eternal God and His Word are great, and that all else is little or is nothing; nay, if it be set against the Most High and His Word is the one frightful thing that the world exhibits." Knox said that he feared the celebration of one idolatrous mass in Scotland more than he feared all the armies of the Frenchmen. He was a true prophet of God. He and his Presbyterian movement were the inspiration for the Puritans in England nearly a century later.

Knox was Calvinistic in his creed. That is to say, he was Pauline. He took the Bible at its face value. He did not trust the church to interpret it. He believed that it meant what it said. In connection with Calvin in Geneva his thinking was clarified so that it made room neither on the right nor the left for theological error. He, along with Douglas and three other ministers, drew up the Scottish confession, which was the forerunner of the Westminster Confession of Faith.

John Knox and Scotland

The work of Knox embodied itself in the church movement called Presbyterianism. Three hundred and fifty years ago the entire Protestant world was Presbyterian in its government. The Waldensian, the Lutheran, the Zwinglian, the Huguenot, the Dutch, the English, and the Scottish churches were all composed on the Presbyterian form of government. This exalted the parity of the clergy by which no bishops or archbishops were to be given dominance, the use of the consistory or the session, the presbytery, the synod, and the general assembly, which was the highest court of appeal. The present form of the Presbyterian Church in the U. S. A. is very similar to those early Presbyterian forms and is directly dependent upon Scottish Presbyterianism both in doctrine and in form.

John Knox was a John the Baptist. He was a pioneer. He had a mission. He was a reformer. He laid the axe to the roots of the trees and left them for another to carve. There was fire in his blood. The hand of God was upon him. Gentler followers would carry on, but Knox was God's man for Scotland in the sixteenth century. He was a man dominated by the truth of God and by the power of his conscience.

The need today is to conserve the spirit of Knox in action, the speech of Knox against sin, the courage of Knox in the pulpit. Had we ministers such as this, authorities and powers would tremble in their presence. And we need the power of conscience to reenforce the Bible teaching among the common people, together with the attitude of the Covenanters, who said, "We, by God's grace, shall with all diligence continually apply our whole power, substance, and our very lives to maintain, set forward, and establish His most blessed Word of God and His congregation, and shall labor at our possibilities to have faithful ministers purely and truly to minister Christ's evangel and sacraments to the people. We shall maintain them and nourish them and defend them, the whole congregation of Christ, and every member thereof, at our whole power, and expending of our whole lives against Satan and the wicked power that does intend tyranny and trouble."

OLIVER CROMWELL AND ENGLAND
OR THE
PROVIDENCE OF GOD

VI

OLIVER CROMWELL AND ENGLAND
OR THE
PROVIDENCE OF GOD

"The Lord reigneth; let the people tremble: he sitteth between the cherubims; let the earth be moved. The Lord is great in Zion; and he is high above all the people."

IT is a terrible and wonderful truth that God governs in the affairs of men. Kings, potentates, and dictators are in His hands. This is especially comforting and reassuring in our own day. It may be most clearly illustrated by the history of England during the Cromwellian period.

Oliver Cromwell was the first Protestant dictator, although his dictatorship was quite different from our modern conception of this term. It is the common and popular practice to cast aspersion upon the character of Cromwell. He is charged with knavery, betraying his cause, personal ambition, cruelty, and with hypocrisy in religion. When visiting Huntingdon I saw the school where Cromwell spent his early days, the church he attended, and the home in which he lived for a short time, but I failed to see any monument to his memory. When Samuel Harden Church wrote his excellent history of Oliver Cromwell he called attention to the fact that though several private monuments had been erected to the memory of Cromwell, no national monument had ever been raised. Since then a bust of Cromwell was placed in the House of Parliament—in 1899—marking the three hundredth anniversary of his birth and restoring him to his rightful place of esteem in the eyes of his countrymen and the world. This delay, no doubt, was due to the intense antipathies to the work and deeds of the Lord Protector which have persisted across the centuries. This intense feeling is still the source of many of these attacks upon Cromwell's character. The bust and portrait of him in Warwick Castle reveal to the observer every trait of a strong, honest, dynamic character, whose straightforwardness and determination would make him many enemies.

The statements of students of Cromwell reveal to us an altogether different picture of his character and career from that held in the popular opinion. Macaulay, who pronounces him the greatest prince who ever ruled in England, says of him, "It is certain that he was to the last honored by his soldiers, obeyed by the whole population of the British Isles, and dreaded by all foreign powers; that he was laid among the ancient sovereigns of England with funeral pomp such as England had never before seen; and that he was succeeded by his son Richard as quietly as any king had ever been succeeded by any prince of Wales." Carlyle says: "From of old, I will confess, this theory of Cromwell's falsity has been incredible to me. Nay, I cannot believe the like, of any great man whatever. No, we cannot figure Cromwell as a Falsity and a Fatuity; the longer I study him and his career, I believe this the less. Why should we? There is no evidence of it ... as a sober industrious farmer, is his life not altogether as that of a true and devout man? He has renounced the world and its ways; its prizes are not the things

that can enrich him. He tills the earth; he reads his
Bible; daily assembles his servants around him to
worship God; he comforts persecuted ministers, is fond
of preachers; nay, can himself preach, exhorts his neighbors to be wise, to redeem the time. In all this what
hypocrisy, ambition, cant, or other falsity? The man's
hopes I do believe were fixed on the other Higher
World; his aim to get well thither by walking well
through his humble course in this world. He courts
no notice: what could notice here do for him? 'Ever
in his Taskmaster's eye' . . . that such a man with
eyes to see, with a heart to dare, should advance from
post to post, from victory to victory, till the Huntingdon
farmer became, by whatever name we might call him,
to be acknowledged the strongest man in England, virtually the king of England, requires no magic to explain it!"

In meeting the charge of massacre of the Irish at
Drogheda and Wexford, when he became dictator,
Samuel Harden Church exonerates Cromwell on the
basis of the war conditions of that time. He believes
that it tended to prevent further effusion of blood because the garrisons were mostly Englishmen who were
making a last stand against the Puritans. Douglas
Campbell, in his exhaustive study of Puritanism, concludes that though men will differ about the character of Cromwell for many generations, the weight of
modern opinion is greatly with Cromwellians.

If, then, we were to try to estimate the character
of Cromwell after these three centuries, it would be
with credit to his name. He was a God-fearing, honest,
earnest Puritan who was pushed by circumstance into
the leadership of the cvil war period of England's
history. We feel that he came there in the providence

of God, that he was the step between the great struggle of William of Orange for religious freedom and the obtaining of that freedom in the tradition of English-speaking countries of the world. John Drinkwater's play, "Oliver Cromwell," historically is accurate when it pictures Cromwell in his home at the close of the day's work, visiting with his friends and then conducting a service of worship with his servants who recently arrived from the fields. Said Cromwell, "Brethren in God, at the end of another day's labor we are met to praise Him from whom are the means to labor and its rewards. As we go about these fields, He is with us. As you deal by me, and I by you, His eye sees us. Nothing good befalls us but that is by His will. No affliction is ours but His loving mercy will hear us. The Lord God walks at our hand. He is here now in our midst. His desires are our freedom, His wrath our tyranny one over another. Be merciful in all your ways, for mercy is His name. May His counsel always be with our little fellowship. If I should fail towards any man, let Him speak. May we be as brothers always, one to another. And may we serve Him to serve whom alone is wisdom. In Jesus Christ's name, Amen."[1] Then they sang, "All people that on earth do dwell."

I. THE PURITAN PICTURE

Puritanism came into being during the reign of Elizabeth but it had its roots back in the entire Reformation movement. The Reformation in England was dissimilar from that in any other country. It has been connected with the name of Henry VIII, that tyrannical and indulgent monarch who symbolizes the efforts of

[1] Drinkwater, John—Oliver Cromwell, Houghton Mifflin Co., Boston

the house of Tudor to revoke the Magna Charta of English liberties. The first we hear of him in connection with the Reformation is his attempt to refute Luther by the publication of a theological treatise. For his effort he was honored by the pope with the title, "The Defender of the Faith." We regret to say that the English Reformation had its material cause in a much more unworthy incident than the German and Swiss Reformations. Henry wished to rid himself of his wife, Catherine of Aragon, who was his brother's widow and the aunt of Philip of Spain, whom he had married under a special dispensation from the pope. She had left him no heir to the throne, and Henry cast his eyes about for a second wife. He settled his choice on Anne Boleyn. When the pope, because of the strength of Philip, refused to annul the marriage, or to declare that it had never been a marriage at all, Henry broke from Rome and set himself up as pope of the English church. The total result of his reign was that the English church became an independent Catholic church with a king as its head. The one beneficial fact accomplished was the placing of the Coverdale Bible in the parish churches during his reign, the four hundredth anniversary of which we celebrated in 1935.

At Henry's death, Edward VI, a twelve-year-old boy, came to the throne. The Prayer Book of 1553 was compiled under him. His advisers were influenced by the Reformed teaching and through their power Calvinism received a foothold in England. John Knox was chaplain to Edward for five years. During his short reign multitudes of the Englishmen became Protestants in fact as well as theory. The church retained the Episcopal form, and hence became Anglican.

But Edward was succeeded by Bloody Mary, who attempted to wipe out the Protestant movement by torture and fire. Thousands of clergy were turned out of office and the leaders of the Protestant movement were put to death. No less than two hundred and seventy-seven suffered martyrdom. But after a few years Mary was succeeded by Queen Elizabeth, who found it desirable and practical to be a Protestant, and for forty years the Anglican church prospered. During this time a large movement of dissatisfaction arose under the name "Puritan."

The Puritans were of three groups—Presbyterians, Non-Conformists, and Independents. The Presbyterian movement was largely the result of the efforts of Knox and Bucer. It became the dominant yeoman and middle-class religion. Side by side with the Presbyterians who desired the Presbyterian to become the state church were the Independents, who held to the independence and supremacy of each individual congregation with the right to call its own ministers. At this time the Acts of Uniformity were passed, and it became illegal for the Independents to meet in their conventicles. The Anglican church began to persecute the Presbyterians and the Independents. Some of the Independents went to the Netherlands, where they might enjoy true liberty of worship. The Presbyterians conformed to the Anglican church for a season.

In this period we see, then, the two extremes: on the one hand Roman Catholicism with absolute control of the religious life of the people; and on the other hand the Independents, who believed in liberty of conscience for all who accepted Christ. In between were the Anglican and the Presbyterian churches, both state churches. They were no more committed to religious freedom than was the Roman church. It was not until Independency took so deep a root in the English religion and its followers became so numerous in the masses of the people that the true spirit of Protestantism flourished. The Roman fallacy, that there must be an earthly head of the church, and that heresy, or choice of opinion, is dangerous to the state, could not be exterminated until the Independent Puritans rose in arms and crushed it, and crushed with it the pretensions of the church and crown to absolute power. Henry, in breaking with Rome, was an actual pope of England. Calvin, severe in spite of his gigantic work for the Reformation, was a pope in Geneva. Luther was a pope in Germany. Knox was a pope in Scotland. These men were all reformers, and as such deserved the grateful esteem of mankind. But it took Cromwell of the Independents to bring freedom of religion, and this influence came largely from the Dutch Republic. The religious factor in the civil war, therefore, consisted of a struggle for freedom of worship.

II. CROMWELL AND CHARLES I

At the death of Elizabeth, James VI, of Scotland, the son of Mary, Queen of Scots, became James I, king of England. He was trained a Presbyterian but gladly followed the Anglican tradition in England because of the deference which the nobility showed to the king, to which he was not accustomed in Scotland. However, greater liberty was given to the dissenting groups, and the Presbyterian representation in Parliament increased. In 1611, the famous King James Version of the Bible was authorized and published. James was succeeded by his son Charles, who had married Henrietta, the sister of Louis XIII and a Catholic Frenchwoman.

Charles found himself between the pressure of this Catholic influence and the check of a Presbyterian parliament that would not grant him money without certain reforms. He attempted to rule without a parliament for eleven years and imposed taxes throughout his country which were thoroughly resisted. The Star Chamber as a court, made up of the king's puppets, inflicted punishments, such as mutilations and tortures, upon those who refused to serve the king. Liberty in England reached a low ebb.

When Charles ascended the English throne, Cromwell, one year his senior, was a farmer at Ely. He had recently been converted through the instrumentality of the Puritans. His conversion was attended by a deep religious experience that shook his life to the foundations and thereinafter made him depend upon God for everything. Cromwell was an intensely human character who liked his wine, his sports, and the village dancing, but he also was honest in his religion. He was selected by his community as a member of the House of Commons and he went to the first parliament of Charles. This parliament was composed mostly of Puritans who were shocked by the vices of the father of Charles, and who were alarmed with the marriage of their new king to a Catholic princess. Therefore, the stage was set for a great struggle.

The youthful king was athletic in frame, dignified in manner, diplomatic in speech, but duplex in his dealings. He was devoted to the theory of divine right of monarchy, and he determined to control his parliament. During this first parliament, Cromwell had the opportunity of witnessing the members in tears, because they foresaw the coming struggle in the nation. They had tried to remove the influence of the unscrupulous Duke of Buckingham but had received a rebuke from their king, and a sad silence descended upon the body. Some attempted to speak and were overcome with passion and forced to sit down. Some spoke in the midst of weeping and tears. Such was Oliver Cromwell's first introduction to parliament, the last parliament that was to be called for eleven years. When he returned in 1638, it was because Charles was compelled to lean upon the people for money. At the same time he tried to strengthen the Episcopacy, and the Presbyterians, fearing a return to Catholicism, joined in a covenant which resulted in the invasion by the Scotch Presbyterians. Then ensued the civil wars. This Puritan rebellion, lasting for four years, was a cruel struggle. The common people, called Roundheads, following a few earls, rallied to the Puritan standard to contend with the nobility, called Cavaliers, who had rallied to the Royal standard, and the war began. Disaster seemed to face the Puritans until gradually Cromwell emerged as the leader of the armies. He recognized that if ever the Puritans were to accomplish anything, the soldiers must be men of religion. He recruited his own army, trained them in their battle formations, insisted on their singing Psalms and praying until the army was really a religious unit. They went into battle singing the Psalms and smiling, believing that God was with them. They became invincible. After the battles of Naseby and Dunbar, Cromwell was the recognized leader of the armies. The king became their captive.

That Cromwell had the good of the nation at heart in his undertakings is evident from his attempt to reconcile Charles and the Parliament for the sake of a constitutional government. In the midst of the conversations, however, it was found that Charles had made a secret treaty with the Presbyterians and with the Scots to establish the monarchy with a Presbyterian state church and no liberty for others. A second civil war ensued and at the close of it the Parliament which remained, consisting only of Independents, condemned the king, and he was executed in 1647. Following this, the last stand of nobles was made in Ireland at Drogheda and Wexford, and Cromwellians crushed it mercilessly, thereby giving rise to the opportunity for criticism on the character of Cromwell.

III. THE PURITAN INFLUENCE ON ENGLAND AND THE WORLD

At first Cromwell attempted to rule with a constitutional Parliament, but the members soon turned back to him the power committed to them. He then became a practical dictator until the year 1658 when he died. The Commonwealth he founded ended with him, and the army invited the son of the beheaded king to the throne. In quick succession Charles II, and his brother James II, ruled over the English people and reverted to the practices of tyranny and of persecution of the Stuart family, so that it was necessary within three decades to invite William III, Prince of Orange, to invade England, to drive out the Stuart family, and to guarantee once and for all that a Catholic sovereign should never sit on the throne of England. At the same time the Bill of Rights was passed which guaranteed the civil liberties of the English people for the future. It is true that Cromwell did not finally establish the religious freedom in which he believed. It was first experienced under his rule, but it was definitely the influence of him and his Puritans that made possible the attainment of it under William III, Prince of Orange.

It was Cromwell who made possible the work of John Wesley and other English revivalists, for he brought the Reformation in England to its logical conclusion. Moreover, the alternative that faced him and John Hampden, his cousin, in 1641 at the beginning of the civil war, faced innumerable others. He had resolved that had the people not responded to the challenge to contend for their liberties he would have sold his property and left England forever. Only a Divine Providence restrained him. An unhistorical incident in Cromwell's life illustrating this was used by James Russell Lowell as the subject of his poem, "A Glance Behind the Curtain." The story is that Cromwell and Hampden, being discouraged by their political efforts, decided to emigrate to America. The vessel in which they had engaged passage was forbidden to sail by an order in council. Cromwell and Hampden are pictured standing on the wharf, considering the advisability of sailing in defiance of the king's order. Hampden speaks:

> *O Cromwell, we are fallen on evil times!*
> *There was a day when England had wide room*
> *For honest men as well as foolish kings:*
> *But now the uneasy stomach of the time*
> *Turns squeamish on them both. Therefore let us*
> *Seek out that savage clime, where men as yet*
> *Are free. . . .*
>
> *Hampden! a moment since my purpose was*
> *To fly with thee—for I will call it flight,*
> *Nor flatter it with any smoother name—*
> *But something in me bids me not to go;*
> *And I am one, thou knowest, who unmoved*
> *By what the weak deem omens, yet give heed*

> *And reverence due to whatsoe'er my soul*
> *Whispers of warning to the inner ear.*
> *Moreover, as I know that God brings round*
> *His purposes in ways undreamed by us,*
> *And makes the wicked but his instruments*
> *To hasten their own swift and sudden fall,*
> *I see the beauty of his providence*
> *In the King's order. . . .*
>
> *Freedom hath yet a work for me to do;*
> *So speaks that inward voice which never yet*
> *Spoke falsely; when it urged the spirit on*
> *To noble deeds for country and mankind.*
>
> *No man is born into the world whose work*
> *Is not born with him . . .*
> *I will have one more grapple with the man*
> *Charles Stuart! . . . What men call luck*
> *Is the prerogative of valiant souls,*
> *The fealty life pays its rightful kings.*
> *The helm is shaking now, and I will stay*
> *To pluck my lot forth; it were a sin to flee.*
>
> *So they two turned together: one to die,*
> *Fighting for freedom on the bloody field;*
> *The other, far more happy, to become*
> *A name earth wears forever next her heart.*

This is exactly what Bradford, Robinson, Williams, and others did when they first left England for the Netherlands, some of whom later left the Netherlands for America. The true background of American Protestantism is dissent. This is the source of our denominational movement. It is the only alternative to a state church. We have come to value this heritage as a great part of our liberty. Whether the state church should be Romanist, Anglican, Presbyterian, or any other, it would ultimately prove itself a despotism. The life of Cromwell saw the coming of the Pilgrims and their reinforcement during the periods of persecution. It also witnessed the writing of the Westminster confession of faith, which doctrinally has been the standard for Presbyterian and Congregational churches.

Cromwell, above others, made England a respected power in the world. The English fleet developed from its beginnings at the time of the destruction of the Spanish Armada under Elizabeth, until it became, under Cromwell, the leading power in the seas. As we scan the history of the world since that time we find the downfall of Spain and absolutist governments that were synonymous with the persecutions of dissenting peoples, while England has become synonymous with those great principles of freedom which later became perfectly embodied in American law. We cannot help but feel that Cromwell, in the providence of God, was the great step between the work of William of Orange, who broke the power of the Inquisition, and the ultimate freedom that we may now enjoy.

In the closing scene of his gripping drama, Drinkwater quotes the last actual words of Cromwell before he died, but he places them in a different setting. Cromwell and his immediate family are in the palace at White-Hall. They are meditating on what has happened through his instrumentality. Cromwell says, "The monarchy will return, I know that." His daughter, Bridget, asks, "Why not always a commonwealth like this, Father?" He replies, "Hereafter there shall be a true commonwealth. We have done that for England. But there must be a king. There is no one to follow me. I am an interlude, as it were. But henceforth kings will be for the defense of this realm, not to use it. That has been our work. . . . I have said a word for freedom, a poor confused word. It was all I could reach to. We are frail with our passions. We are beset." Then he and Bridget stand beside the bedside of the aged mother of Cromwell and he prays, "Thou hast made me, though very unworthy, a mean instrument to do the people some good, and Thee service. And many of them have set too high a value upon me, though others wish and would be glad of my death. But, Lord, however Thou dost dispose of me, continue and go on to do good for them. Give them one heart and mutual love. Teach those who look too much upon thine instrument to depend more upon Thyself. Pardon such as desire to trample upon the dust of a poor worm, for they are Thy people, too. And pardon the folly of this short prayer, even for Jesus Christ's sake."[1]

And this is Cromwell, a willing servant in the Providence of God as He overturns the course of nations.

God works in a mysterious way
His wonders to perform;
He plants His footsteps in the sea
And rides upon the storm.

---
[1] Drinkwater, John—Oliver Cromwell, Houghton Mifflin Co., Boston

ROGER WILLIAMS
AND AMERICA
OR
THE GENIUS OF PROTESTANTISM

VII

ROGER WILLIAMS AND AMERICA
OR
THE GENIUS OF PROTESTANTISM

"A voice crying in the wilderness."

ROGER WILLIAMS was the prophet of soul liberty. His struggle to secure this principle for the inhabitants of the new world has given him immortality. He is one of the great figures of American history. Like other prophets he was persecuted by his own generation but honored by their posterity. We might compare Williams to Moses, Elijah, or John the Baptist. His voice was almost solitary in the wilderness of his day as it was lifted to make straight the way for soul liberty. In England and in America, toleration was practically unknown and any man who would set himself against the trend of his day was bound to be misunderstood but also to be great. There is no extant picture of Williams, so that we cannot be certain of his physical appearance. Yet Rhode Island has fashioned two important statues of him in the likeness of his oldest male descendant. Those statues present him as a vigorous man in his early thirties dressed in the knee breeches and long cloak of the Puritan times, with a sturdy figure and an intelligent looking but determined countenance. Governor Winthrop of the Bay Colony spoke of him on his arrival as "a godly minister." Williams had come to America in order that he might have freedom of conscience, and he sacrificed many earthly preferments to follow the leadings of his conscience. He was steadfast in his purposes and once having formed an opinion upon a great principle, all of the logic of John Cotton and the eloquence of Thomas Hooker could not move him from his position. Though Williams was possessed by limitations of character, as is every man, he deserves his place in the American Hall of Fame, and in particular in relation to the spiritual life.

We are speaking upon the subject of Roger Williams because in him the great Protestant Reformation reached the end of the dialectic process. This development of thought was simultaneous with the founding of Providence Plantations, which became the first State in America to guarantee complete freedom in religion or absolute soul liberty. In 1936, as the celebrations of this founding of Providence Plantations were proceeding, the governor of the commonwealth of Massachusetts met the governor of the State of Rhode Island and formally delivered to him a resolution adopted by the 1936 general court of Massachusetts repealing the sentence of banishment passed in 1636 on Roger Williams. We might think when first reading about this gracious act, though somewhat belated in its execution, that the principle for which Williams sacrificed all has triumphed in America. The purpose of our study will be to examine whether that be true.

The life of Williams was one of the most romantic and adventurous of the early colonists. He was an Englishman by birth. Some claim that Wales was his native section, and opinions differ as to whether he was born in 1601 or 1607. At an early age Sir Edward Coke became interested in him because he de-

voted some of his time to taking notes in shorthand
of the speeches in the Star Chamber. Coke was one
of the first directors of the Charterhouse School, and
he obtained a scholarship for Roger in that institution
which was to send out so many great characters, including John Wesley. After several years Roger entered Pembrook College, Cambridge, and began the
study of law. After his graduation, his attention turned
to theology and he diligently studied the Scriptures.
It was through this that his conscience was aroused
to oppose the common church practices of his day.
He became a separatist, or a non-conformist. Placing
himself on the side of the Puritans, he soon found
himself in conflict with the established church and
especially Archbishop Laud, who was seeking out these
non-conformists for persecution. Roger knew that
within a reasonably short time he would be hailed before the Star Chamber, which was administering those
severe punishments of mutilation and death. He fled,
taking with him his wife Mary, and they finally succeeded in sailing for America where they arrived in
1631. Instead of finding freedom of speech and conscience in the colonies, Roger was amazed to see that
the Massachusetts churches not only retained their con-
nections with the Church of England but also had established as intolerant a church organization on the
Puritan lines as was the Church of England on Anglican
lines. Before long he was in controversy with the
leaders of the church. At first he was honored and
offered high positions. These he refused because of
his principles. During a period of five years he was
variously assistant in the Salem church, instructor in
the Plymouth church, and then teacher and pastor of
the Salem church. It was in Salem that he came into

conflict with the elders of the Boston community. He was summoned before the council and examined several times. Finally, the sentence of banishment was passed upon him; he was to be deported to England. His friend, Governor Winthrop, advised him that there was land free from charter to the south and west of Plymouth and the Bay Colony and that he could carry on his work there. So in the dead of winter, Williams and five companions made their departure and after fourteen weeks of hardship landed at Narraganset Bay and founded Providence Plantations because of the beneficent providences of God which led them there. The State which was to rise on those foundations was to be the first to declare its independence from England and the last to ratify the United States' Constitution, and finally only did so when a bill of rights was appended thereto.

The principle governing Williams' life and finding expression in the State of "Rhode Island and Providence Plantations" is that of soul liberty, or the right to dissent. In the statue of Williams a book is held in the left arm and across that book, which resembles the Bible, is written, "Soul Liberty." This is the doctrine that the state shall have power "in civil things only." The individual is to have perfect freedom of religion and of speech so long as he does not disturb the peace of the state and transgress the rights of others. In this doctrine the Reformation reached its conclusion. Not only was religious liberty from the dominant communions granted but soul liberty in an absolute sense. This has become a cardinal principle of American life, but it is a principle in danger of being denied to us in these days. It should be helpful to us then to examine the position of Williams in regard to oaths, to the relation of church and state, and to the subject of liberty.

I. WILLIAMS' POSITION IN REGARD TO OATHS

The cause of the controversy that raged about Williams found its source in his attitude toward oaths. While a young man and greatly in need of funds, Williams cast aside the opportunity for a large inheritance because he would not swear an oath of allegiance in the English courts. Later he found great difficulty in sailing to America because an oath of loyalty was exacted from every emigrant. He also refused to swear any oath when he came to the new country. He contended that an oath should never be required from an unregenerate man since an oath is an act of worship, and worship cannot be forced. In one aspect this seems merely a curious and harmless opinion. What he desired is now allowed in every state in America. Law permits us to affirm when we conscientiously object to taking an oath. He stoutly refused to pledge loyalty to anything that did not fully accord with his principles. When this position was added to his criticism of the Massachusetts church for not abjuring all connection with the English church, to his argument that the Massachusetts charter was invalid because the land was not purchased from the Indians, and to the declaration that the civil magistrate has no right to punish breeches of the first table of the Decalogue, which relates to man's duties to God, Williams found himself in a difficult position in relation to the Massachusetts Colony.

We have said that Massachusetts has recently revoked this banishment of Williams. Following this the question was raised in one of our leading national periodicals of present freedom of conscience. The author called to our attention under the title, "The Ghost of Roger Williams," the fact that in the same year members of a Massachusetts college were forced to resign their posts, that an honor student in a Massachusetts college was forced to forswear his degree, and that parents of children in the Massachusetts schools were forced to undergo arrest and trial, all in the name of freedom of conscience. The author, Mr. Paul Hutchison, reminded us that twenty-six states already have laws requiring some form of test oath for teachers and that the American Legion is attempting to make such oaths universal. He reminded us of the case of Dr. Douglas Clyde Macintosh, who applied for American citizenship and was refused. His case came before the Supreme Court. When Dr. Macintosh was asked if he would bear arms in any war in which the country might be involved, he replied that he would bear arms in any war that his conscience held just. Dr. Macintosh is not a pacifist. He served in the Canadian and American armies in the World War. He demanded the right to obey his conscience in this matter. The Supreme Court denied his right to citizenship on the following basis: "When he [Dr. Macintosh] speaks of putting his allegiance to the will of God above his allegiance to the government, it is evident . . . that he means to make his own interpretation of the will of God the decisive test . . . We are a nation with a duty to survive; a nation whose constitution contemplates war as well as peace; whose government must go forward on the assumption, and can safely proceed on no other, that unqualified allegiance to the nation and submission and obedience to the laws of the land, as well those made for war as those made for peace, are not inconsistent with the will of God." Said Hutchison, "That decision . . . means that, under the Constitution, the loyal citizen of the United States must accept a vote of Congress as in accordance with the will of God. What becomes of the individual's rights of conscience in such a state?"

Williams' principle is consistent with loyalty to our national government though it will not admit of oaths. Williams held that while in an organization it is necessary to obey the rules and laws of that organization, but that no power can compel one to remain in that organization if because of conscience he desires to withdraw. If one desires the protection of the American state he must yield obedience to that state and he must accept the laws of that state as authoritative. A democracy is different from a form of government in which the people have no voice in making their laws. When the representatives of the people legislate for them the individuals must bow to this law. Of course the right to resistance is always retained, but with the exception of this any other course would result in anarchy.

We must not confuse freedom of conscience in religious matters with political obligation. The decision of the Supreme Court does not establish a totalitarian conception of the state, which gives Congress the right to legislate in matters of religious freedom. A glance at the system in Russia or Germany will clarify this difference. In the Russian state, the church is considered an enemy to progress. Personal religious life is detrimental to revolutionary, social, family and national changes. Therefore, it must be obliterated. In its place atheism is established as a state religion. Forced conformity to this theory is experienced in the life of every member of the Communist party. In Germany is a totalitarian state of another kind; the state presses its claim to control the economic, educational, and religious life of the people. It has invaded the sphere of private belief and legislated concerning the faith of the people. The case of Dr. Martin Niemoller presents the example of one singled out for persecution because he refused to abandon his Christian faith and his freedom to preach. The increase in the number of totalitarian states and of the influence of the idea governing them in other countries is caused by the insecurity of our times. The dictators promise to the people security, employment, and prosperity in return for total allegiance. The price of freedom of conscience is paid for this security. Our danger is that the same causes will lead us to commit more and more of individual phases of life to the government and it ultimately will deny us our precious privilege of freedom of conscience.

It was a similar sense of insecurity which caused the Puritans of Massachusetts to banish Williams and to deny this principle. The new state was seeking a foothold in a new country and needed peace. Enemies were working in the mother country to gain a revocation of the Bay Colony's charter. Had any disturbance within the colony risen to give occasion to political or ecclesiastical enemies in England, Massachusetts Colony might have suffered severely. It preferred to sacrifice Williams and his principle rather than its own security. This has often been forgotten in evaluating the Puritan action.

II. WILLIAMS AND THE CHURCH

The principle enunciated by Williams in regard to the church is absolute separation from the state. Because of this principle Williams refused to be a teacher in the Boston congregation. Perhaps we should know something of the condition of this early Commonwealth. John Cotton was the leading divine in the congregation. He established a theocracy on Old Testament principles by which the state had power to enforce not only civil but also religious law. Laws were enacted regarding the worship of God, and observance of the Sabbath, as well as the civil matters of murder, adultery, and thievery. When the church tried a man and condemned him, the state executed the sentence. The principle was the same one that operated back of the inquisition of the Roman church and the Calvinistic government of Geneva, and of the English state church. The Independents were the first to proclaim this principle of separation, and Williams was a consistent Independent. When the members of the New England state succeeded in escaping from England and founding their new country, they did not wish to make it a haven for all of the unclean birds of Europe, so they made a state just as intolerant along their way of thinking as any of the previous conditions in Europe had been. Those who did not conform to their law were banished. Illustrations of this are Anne Hutchinson and Roger Williams.

The true Anglo-American tradition, ultimately expressed in Williams' new State of "Rhode Island and Providence Plantations," of complete religious freedom was brought to America by the Pilgrims in 1620. These were Independent Puritans who had been expelled from England under Elizabeth because of the Acts of Uniformity. They found refuge in the Netherlands in Leyden and Amsterdam. There they imbibed the principles of soul liberty won by William of Orange and guaranteed in the Union of Utrecht. This was the conviction of Bradford and Brewster. Opposed to it were the Presbyterian Puritans who came in large numbers between 1629 and 1640 to the Bay Colony. They believed in a state church, reformed but without toleration. The concept of toleration made its way gradually from Plymouth to Salem and from Salem to the other Bay Colony churches. It was not till 1674 that Baptists were permitted in the Colony and much later was this toleration granted to other sects, such as Quakers. All dissenters were banished.

Against this tendency of uniting the church and state Williams took his stand. The truth he declared seems commonplace to us. It is embodied in every court in every State of our Union. It is accepted by every religious denomination in our Republic. Williams stoutly affirmed that man's relation to his Maker is altogether above and beyond the power of the state. To worship God under compulsion hurts the soul. Williams believed that the church had a right to declare the commandments and revelation of God but no right to enforce them. For a time, at every session of the general court, the young minister was reproved or enjoined. At last, in 1635, the specific charges were formulated and he was banished, or as John Cotton said, "enlarged," out of Massachusetts.

Is the position of Williams in regard to the church and state, which has been such a fundamental of our modern thinking, endangered today? Are there any evidences of a return to state support or control of the church? According to the press, Dr. Samuel M. Shoemaker, the American leader of the Oxford Group Movement, has come out with just such a plea. He said, "It seems to me that any government which has the people's interests at heart has the right and the duty to ask whether their religion, as the churches preach and practice it, is genuinely beneficial to the people. We liberal-minded Americans see the danger which inheres in any interference by the state in religion. We do not see the danger in allowing to go on unchecked and unchallenged almost any church, however corrupt it may be in morals, and however meddlesome in politics. We really want the state to take the responsibility for keeping things in order, so that we may continue our religious practice as we wish." This statement was issued close upon Frank Buchman's own praise of Hitler as the Savior of Europe. In commenting upon this a brilliant religious editor asked, "What does this mean? Only one thing, if it is logically carried out, namely, the rule of the churches and of religion by the state, and that is precisely what is being attempted in Germany, in Spain, in Mexico, and in Russia. To give the state authority to decide what is good religion and what constitutes a good church is to throw civilizaion back into benighted monarchism, which is what we have as a matter of fact in present day dictatorships."

A few years ago such state control of religion was on the wane, but now voices in favor of it are rising on every hand. At the close of the last century the greatest amount of tolerance that the world has seen existed, but today it is being repudiated. Liberalism today is on the wane. Soul liberty is greatly in danger. Roger Williams' thesis, "Live and Let Live," is being rapidly discarded.

III. WILLIAMS' POSITION ON SOUL LIBERTY

In brief, soul liberty means absolute freedom for all beliefs. It is the right of all to freedom of worship or lack of worship. It means the privilege of dissent.

Williams believed that Jews, Turks, Catholics, and Protestants, all had a perfect right to their own religious opinions, provided they did not interfere with others. As a result the Compact of Providence related to civil matters only. There are three possible positions regarding civil and religious authority. We may affirm the duty of the government to support and control the institutions of religion. We may affirm as a concession to human weakness the expediency of tolerating false views of religion. Or we may affirm the absolute wrong of any interference by the government in matters of religious faith. The second theory is called toleration; the third is the position of soul liberty. It is the position that the government must refrain from tolerance and intolerance and leave the consciences of all men free. In his volume, *The Bloody Tenet of Persecution*, Williams declares that the "great cause of the indignation of the Most High against the state and country is . . . that all others descending from them, whether Jews or Gentiles, have not been allowed civil cohabitation with them, but have been distressed and persecuted by them." Roger Williams wanted equal rights for the Turk and the atheist as well as for himself, a strict Calvinist believer.

The accusation has been made that this principle will destroy law and order. Williams answered that accusation with a lucid and cogent expression of the essential doctrine of civil liberty and true democracy. It is in the form of the parable of a ship. He said, "There goes many a ship to sea, with many hundred souls in one ship, whose weal or woe is common and is a true picture of a commonwealth or a human combination of society. It hath fallen out sometime that both Papists and Protestants, Jews and Turks, may be embarked on one ship, upon which supposal I do affirm that all the liberty of conscience that I ever pleaded for turns on these two hinges, that none of the Papists, Protestants, Jews, or Turks be forced to come to the ship's prayers for worship, if they practice it. I further add that I never denied that notwithstanding this liberty, the commander of the ship ought to command the ship's course, yea, and also to command that justice, peace, and sobriety be kept and practiced, both among the shipmen and all the passengers. If any of the seamen refuse to perform their service or passengers pay their freight, if any refuse to help in person or in purse toward the common charge and defense, if any refuse to obey the common laws and orders of the ship, concerning their common peace or preservation, and if any shall mutiny and rise against their commanders and officers, if any should preach or write that there ought to be no commanding officers because all are equal in Christ, therefore no masters, no officers, no laws, no corrections, no punishment; I say I never deny it, but in such cases whatever is pretended, the commander or commanders may judge, resist, compel, and punish such transgressors to their deserts and merits." This is soul liberty in harmony with the laws of the state.

This position resulted in certain problems in Providence itself. It was not long before one Arnold appeared in Providence who became a nuisance to the State and did so because of the freedom of his conscience. The Providence government solved the problem by refusing voting privileges to him until his conscience became enlightened. His conscience was in conflict with the welfare of the other members of society. That conflict still arises and in our day we have need for men of the stripe of Roger Williams constantly to inject vigor into the state by obeying their conscience regardless of the cost. Williams himself has probably given us the correct dividing line between authority of conscience and the authority of the state.

While in an organization it is necessary for us to obey the rules and laws of that organization, there is no power under heaven able to compel us to remain in that organization if because of our conscience we desire to withdraw. This is a right guaranteed to us in the Constitution of the United States. May that right of soul liberty be preserved.

We need modern Roger Williamses to guarantee the benefits of the struggle of the centuries to us. We must permit liberty for Jews, Catholics, Protestants, and atheists. The right to differ and to have freedom for dissent is our Protestant heritage. Let such prophets remember that they may expect persecution from their own generation but honor from the generations to come. Let them remember John the Baptist, who died in the dungeon but who was greater than all those born of woman.

WHITHER PROTESTANTISM?
OR
INDEPENDENCY AND UNION

VIII

WHITHER PROTESTANTISM?
OR
INDEPENDENCY AND UNION

"Stand fast, therefore, in the liberty wherewith Christ hath made us free, and be not entangled again with the yoke of bondage."

WHAT price liberty! It has been at tremendous cost over a period of five and a half centuries that we have obtained our right to dissent. Absolute freedom of conscience is our heritage. Strange it is that the development process of the Reformation ideas ended where it started in its first representative, John Wycliffe. Wycliffe was born about the year 1324 and his Reformation activity and preaching took place about 1377. From him the torch was passed to Huss, the Bohemian, and from Huss it went to Luther and then through the process which is now known to us. We might take a summary of the teaching of Wycliffe from a recent book entitled, *The Religious Background of American Culture,* by Thomas Cuming Hall:

"Wycliffe did not attack the mass itself; he was at mass when the stroke came that heralded his death. He did something more dangerous; he took from it for the ordinary man all magic and external power. Preaching, he said, was more important than the sacrament and the body of Christ no longer lay upon the altar as the center of worship. The logic of his position was never more tersely expressed than by Emerson long after, who probably knew little of Wycliffe, when he said that the sacrament had simply ceased to interest him. The church building ceased all of a sudden to be a temple and became a conventicle. Cathedral and minister were no longer shelters for the Highest, lying in state upon the altar, but convenient places of assembly to hear preaching and to make room for prayer. For the common man Wycliffe swept away even more effectually than Luther and Calvin the whole historic church, for in its place he put the individual interpretation of the English Bible by every simple reader. The historic priesthood lost all meaning, for every Christian was a priest before God and was under obligation so far as he had gifts and strength to proclaim the Word of God. The forgiveness of sin had nothing to do with either the magic of a sacrament or the message of a minister, but depended solely upon the calling of God to life and duty; and only in the faithful fulfillment of that duty could one make his calling and election sure. The sinner could not earn it, but he could by loving service come to realize that God had called and that he had come. Every soul could and must come into God's presence without mediation of either priest or church. Salvation rested upon no external ceremony, but solely upon a change of heart, to which God called all men, and to which all the elect would respond. The pope himself could not be sure of salvation, save as he lived the life of love, and many popes had made evident by their lives that they were probably not saved."[1]

Wycliffe emphasized preaching. He exalted the Bible in the language of the people. He insisted that

---
[1] Hall, Thomas Cuming, **The Religious Background of American Culture**, Little Brown and Co., Boston

the sacraments are representative only and he demanded an ethical manifestation of one's Christianity. He was in the Pauline-Augustinian tradition, and his creed was essentially the same as Calvin's, one hundred and fifty years before Calvin's day, with the exception of Calvin's emphasis upon the church and the Episcopal ministry. Wycliffe may properly be called the father of the Anglo-American Protestantism. It was in the Wycliffian tradition, which derived its faith and inspiration directly from the Bible, that Oliver Cromwell, William III, Prince of Orange, John Wesley, General Booth, Charles Finney, and D. L. Moody came. The theology of each was derived from the New Testament, and their doctrine of God, of the Trinity, of the sacrifice of Christ, of the Holy Spirit, of justification in Christ, of the sacrifice of the cross, of eternal life and heaven for the justified, and of pains in hell for the damned, were practically identical, revealing that the New Testament teaching is clear upon these facts.

The drama of Wycliffe's life is quite as interesting as that of the later reformers. He was expelled from Oxford, brought to trial before the church hierarchy, was the object of papal bulls, was protected by the soldiers of John of Gaunt, but finally died, still within the church. The seriousness of the movement to return to primitive Christianity that he started was not fully realized in his day. It was two hundred and fifty years later in the work of Roger Williams that the Anglo-American tradition was brought back to Wycliffe. Dissent is the key to that tradition.

Each individual may stop where he wishes in his practical application of this Reformation development, but he may not stop where he wishes in the logic of the matter. Neither Luther nor Calvin went as far as

Wycliffe. Luther guarded the historic church, calling it by another name. Calvin guarded the historic teaching ministry. Both of them, along with Zwingli, failed to grasp the principle of separation of church and state. Huss was a Wycliffite, and Luther in the debate with Eck admitted that he was a Hussite on Bible authority. This became the formal cause of the Reformation, whereas justification by faith was the material cause. Knox brought the element of conscience, awakened by the Word, to the forefront. Christian liberty was only a by-product in the time of the reformers, and it was not realized in the theological groups. It remained for the political reformers to apply the Protestant doctrine. William of Orange first procured Christian liberty through the civil wars of the Netherlands. Luther, Zwingli, Calvin, and Knox were unwilling to grant soul liberty. Cromwell was an independent, accepting the Reformation and permitting each group of believers to be bound by their own covenant, with no governmental or ecclesiastical interference. He brought toleration to pass, but a state religion ensued. Roger Williams was the one to lay the foundation for true soul liberty and the final application of Protestant principles. His work became incorporated and expressed in the American heritage.

One may stop in this dialectic with a practical application of part of this group of truths at a state church, a creedal church, or he may follow the process through to independency. In independency each church has its own covenant or constitution with a voluntary membership. It will continue as long as its ministry and message appeal to the hearts of the people.

We contend then that in logic the last word in Protestantism leaves us with the principle of independence. In practice we have observed that this presents many difficulties as well as advantages. Some of these difficulties are being faced by a committee of Greater Boston Congregationalism to bring about a closer unity and concord among the independent churches which dominate this area, that a stronger impact may be made upon the community. Yet to find a basis for such co-operation seems almost futile because of the rugged independency of each group. The Park Street Church is in this tradition. It has its own constitution. It is answerable to no one but its own congregation and it stands squarely in the Wycliffian tradition, as it has been purchased for us. Let us examine some of the implications of this principle of independency.

I. THE MEANING OF THIS PRINCIPLE TO ECCLESIASTICAL ORGANIZATIONS

When we apply this principle to the ecclesiastical organizations in reference to membership, ordination, and boards and agencies, we have some illuminating facts concerning our position and our activity.

Membership in an ecclesiastical organization becomes purely voluntary. Williams' principle might be stated as follows: While in an organization it is necessary for a person to obey the laws and rules of that organization, but there is no power that is able to compel him to remain in that organization if his conscience and the Word of God advise him to withdraw. This is the principle of independency. It is the teaching that we are not saved by membership in a church but by membership in the great invisible Church, which is the body of Christ. This does some very radical things to the idea of the church as an organization. The Protestant tradition says that membership in the true Church is spiritual. It is God's work to purge a dead conscience and quicken it to obedience to His Word. No man can judge who is a member of the Church. The only norms we have are the works that man performs and the confession he makes. We may say that a man does not bear fruit of his confession but we cannot finally judge whether he is a true believer. However, each church organization has the right by its covenant or its constitution to set up the requirements for its own membership, provided nobody is compelled to unite with it. This gives every group of people the privilege of representing and perfecting its freedom of conscience in a social form, Hence our many denominations. Denominationalism has its root in the Protestant tradition.

Apply this principle to the clergy of the church. What constitutes true ordination? The Anglican church, which is reformed in some measure, believes that ordination is valid only through the laying on of hands of the bishop in apostolic succession. This is the same principle as in the Church of Rome, that is that the true Church consists of clergymen, bishops, archbishops, cardinals, the pope, who is the vicar of Christ, and the sacraments. Wycliffe and the reformers when they reached their logical conclusion swept this away with their great principle of the priesthood of the believer and mediatorial work of the Lord Jesus Christ. The attitude of most Protestant denominations even today is that only ordained men have the right to serve the sacrament. Though these churches do not believe in apostolic succession, they permit only those men empowered by the organization to mediate the sacraments of the Lord's Supper and Baptism. Hereby a precious truth is lost, for most certainly Wycliffe was right in using what were called "poor preachers" or laymen, in which he was later followed by Wesley and Booth and Moody, not only to preach but also to serve the sacrament. Reserving the privilege of serving the sacrament to ordained men who are out of the apostolic succesion can only be justified by expediency, that is, the need of law and order. A third attitude common today is the irregular ordination of unequipped men in missions and tabernacles to the gospel ministry. These then assume the title of "Reverend." What shall we say constitutes true ordination?

If the Protestant Reformation is right, ordination must be by the Holy Spirit, who alone is able to call and anoint a man for spiritual service. It is not a matter of apostolic succession through the laying on of hands or the matter of the authorization of an organization. In both of these tragic mistakes in ordination have resulted. True succession to the primitive Apostles and Church can come only through being joined to that Church by the Holy Spirit and called to such an office. It is perfectly proper that denominations or independent churches should put limitations upon the men whom they set apart for the office of the ministry. A high standard should be kept in moral and spiritual and intellectual requirements, but all the ordinations possible will never make some men ministers of God. Whence then comes the authority of a minister and his message? Is it from the historic church or from any organization? We maintain that the authority of a man's message must come from the witness of the Holy Ghost to the preaching of the Word in the heart of the individual who hears it. If that witness is lacking, all the blue laws, the Inquisitions, and the church constitutions will be unavailing. God alone can and God must do the work. Therefore, the authority of the minister comes primarily from the Word of God and from the Third Person of the Trinity speaking through him to the hearts of those who hear him. Secondary authority may be organizational.

What is the implication of this principle in reference to the boards and agencies of denominations? We have witnessed in the last decade a terrible shake-up in this realm. The shaking is still going on until we wonder what will be left. It is pitiable to watch the frantic efforts of board secretaries, college presidents, and agency representatives to stop the retrenching and retreating of their organizations. It has the appearance of attempting to keep schools, colleges, and organizations operating on a particular line that has lost its appeal. The church is now trying to do with high pressure salesmanship and campaigns what it once did with heart interest. Therefore, some denominations that have organizational authority compel by devious means the individual churches to continue to support certain works in which they are not interested. If the true principle of independency were applied, what is not of God would die. As a result some colleges supported by Christian gifts and teaching anti-Christian theories would immediately end their career of destruction. Likewise, returned missionaries would make the appeal for their own work, instead of board secretaries. If these missionaries have the fire of God such as did Adoniram Judson, William Carey, and Hudson Taylor, the money will be forthcoming. If not, the work deserves to die. Metaphorically it is time to kill the secretaries. It is time to remove them from mediating between the field workers and the churches. Instead of the Christian church's being burdened from above by hierarchies and committees and organizations that are demanding support, it should have its inspiration from below. All Christian movements have their rise in Christian hearts instead of something that is foisted upon the individual life by an organization. The logic of dissent would bring an end to many practices now pervading the church denominations. It would not end the missionary and benevolent enterprise but would afford a freer channel for it to seek its correct level.

II. THE MEANING OF THIS PRINCIPLE IN RELATION TO DENOMINATIONALISM

Concerning denominations we must consider the doctrine of the Church. We have already stated the idea that considers the church as an organization of one form or another in which a person is saved and out of which he is lost. As opposed to this the Protestant doctrine, and we believe the Bible teaching, is that the Church is formed of called-out ones, of the elect who are true believers, born again and making up Christ's body. These may or may not be members of the same organization but nevertheless are members of the Church. No pope nor hierarchy of any kind, whether Roman Catholic or Protestant, can be substituted for this organism. Because of this doctrine of the Church we have no fear for the Church in spite of the disintegrating tendency in the denominations of our day. We have called to our attention constantly the seeming apostacy in the church and the disinterest of the church's members. This in turn has driven men to think of union of various church organizations, and many such unions are being promoted at the present moment. All such unions or lack of them can never change what constitutes the true Church, for wherever two meet together in the name of Christ is the Church, that is, when two come together who have His nature. This, then, is His body, indwelt by His Holy Spirit and accomplishing His redeeming work in the world today as Jesus Himself did the redeeming work of God when on earth. Against this Church the gates of hell cannot prevail and the fires of persecution are harmless.

Let us consider this principle as applied to interchurch work. In the business world we have a doctrine of laissez-faire, that is, a hands-off policy, which permits competition to bring various businesses to their correct level. If one business has a competitor with a better product at a more reasonable price, it is compelled to meet this competition or fail. Independency implies a laissez-faire policy in spiritual things. If every individual church were but voluntarily associated with other churches and were independent in itself the number of churches and strength of churches would soon be reached by competition. That is, if there were three churches at one roadway intersection of a village, which needed only one or two, the natural process would cause the people to gravitate to the church in which they received the spiritual help they desired. Gradually the church not needed would be forced out of operation. Instead of that, we have vested interests of large denominations subsidizing those churches in order to keep all of them operating for the purpose of propagating certain denominational interests. Independency would remove such vested interests and it would be only a matter of time until the correct level was reached. If, however, these three churches were compelled to unite by a union of the denominations, it would rob the people of their privilege of dissent.

Consider the meaning of this principle in relationship to the church union movement. Divisions and denominations have been called "crimes," "disgraces," "hindrances," "blocks to progress." There is a great call going forth to organizational union today, which may be illustrated from many denominations. The tendency in many instances is to bring about organizational union at the expense of principle. We can see no reason at all why there could not be unions between various groups from whom the cause for separation has disappeared, but to consider those who refuse to join such a union because of principles, bigots or hindrances to progress, is to fail to comprehend the fundamental principle of Protestantism.

What is the purpose of the union movement of our day? Are we to have a second Roman Catholic Church for the purpose of competing with Roman Catholicism? To this we believe most unionists would reply in the negative. Then is the union movement for the purpose of having one great church in the world as an organizational unit that it may by legislation or force compel evil-doers and dissenters to obey its precepts? If so, the short-cut to such a process is to renounce the Reformation and return to Romanism now. At the Oxford Conference the presiding archbishop regretted that Rome sent no official delegate to its discussions and meetings. Are we to infer that the tendency of these union movements is a return to Rome or at least to Rome's principles? That would imply that the Reformation was a great mistake and that the tens of thousands who suffered and died for our heritage did so in vain.

Think of what a Protestant union would mean. First, it would mean forced uniformity. Several of the great denominations most actively talking union have in the last decade proved by their official acts that they will not tolerate dissent in their membership in reference to the support of missionary and benevolent enterprises. Human nature is such that, given the opportunity to exercise such power, oppression of dissenting minorities would again arise. Where then is our cardinal American principle? Secondly, we believe that such a union would cause individuals to be allied with a group whose convictions they do not share. This is true now in reference to the Federal Council of Churches. Many churches would like to belong to this organization but do not for the simple reason that the Council too often expresses itself authoritatively on matters diametrically opposed to the conviction of these churches. Moreover, it fosters a certain type of Christianity quite foreign to the Reformation truths. Third, we believe that a widespread Protestant union in America would mean the suppression of our precious principle of soul liberty, or dissent. Therefore, as we examine historic Protestantism we believe that true union must be in Spirit and in truth. It exists now between believers regardless of their denominational background. Truly Catholic spirits find fellowship with others of like mind regardless of their organizational connection. Christ never contemplated a number of little Roman churches in the form of denominations with the practice of aping the college of cardinals and the pope. Christ prayed for a true unity in the midst of all the dissent possible in human personality.

III. THE MEANING OF THIS PRINCIPLE IN RELATION TO OUR COUNTRY

The privilege of the dissenting mind in America means the retaining of the cardinal principle of our

Whither Protestantism? 139

national heritage in the division of the church and state as against returning to the despotic and foreign condition from which Protestantism saved us. The union of church and state with the doctrine of "exterminating heresy by exterminating the heretics" is still the fundamental principle of Roman Catholicism. To this, no thinking man could wish to turn. The past has taught us from the long struggles of Lutheranism, Genevan Presbyterianism, Anglicanism, and even Methodism, that we dare not trust a uniform Protestant church to give true liberty or even toleration. Dissent has been the genius of American Protestantism since Williams' principle was added to the Constitution and it is essential to our continuance in this great heritage and tradition.

The dissenting mind means the keeping of soul liberty in our country. We do not call for bigotry, nor prejudice, nor strife with any other sect that might choose to exist in our country. We do not call for any suppression nor for any intolerance. If any theory which does not contemplate the overthrow of regular government can gain a following, we say with Gamaliel, "Let them alone: for if this counsel or this work be of men, it will come to naught: but if it be of God, ye cannot overthrow it; lest haply ye be found even to fight against God." We demand a right, according to the dissenting mind, for each sect and person to express himself as he will within the bounds of decency, sobriety, and order. The dissenting mind demands the right of liberty for our conscience according to the Word of God, within or without a church.

We believe that freedom for dissent in religion and freedom in civic life go hand in hand. If Protestantism fails America is doomed. The odds within the churches and in the popular mind seem to be against the Reformation principles today. The tendencies are in the opposite direction, but the tradition of the dissenting mind is a fundamental basic background of Anglo-American Protestantism and we have the conviction that it will make itself felt in spite of the present tendencies. It is time, however, for Protestants to awake. By our vote, by our church support and membership, by our actions, we must resist all encroachments upon our liberty and our heritage.

Where does this lead me as an individual? In these discussions we have been thinking out loud. We trust the thought has been clear and logical. We make no claim to inerrancy. Perhaps there is a fallacy somewhere in our argument, but we wish to be heard in defense of what we consider our "goodly heritage." We do not follow our logic all the way to independency. We stop with a creedal Presbyterianism, which we believe is voluntary and Biblical, but which must grant within its bounds liberty from any compulsory support for sections of denominational work which might conceivably not be in harmony with its creed. This we hold to be consistent with the Protestant principle of voluntary alliance with any church. So long as the Spirit and Word testify to its work and it permits liberty, it embodies this Protestant truth, but if it should refuse that liberty or if any other denomination of which we were a member should, we should be compelled to go to the next step, which would be utter independency. You, in turn, may stop in the process where your conscience permits you to rest, and we will grant the privilege to you as a right under the principle of the dissenting mind.

www.ingramcontent.com/pod-product-compliance
Lightning Source LLC
Chambersburg PA
CBHW071442160426
43195CB00013B/1999